S0-AEC-693

People development in developing countries

People development in developing countries

ROSS MATHESON

A HALSTED PRESS BOOK

JOHN WILEY & SONS
New York–Toronto

187307

331.11
m 427

All Rights Reserved. No part of this publication may be reproduced, stored in a retrieval system or transmitted in any form or by any means: electronic, electrostatic, magnetic tape, mechanical, photocopying, recording or otherwise, without permission in writing from the publishers.

English language edition, except U.S.A. and Canada published by Associated Business Programmes Ltd
17 Buckingham Gate, London SW 1

Published in the U.S.A. and Canada by Halsted Press, a Division of John Wiley & Sons Inc., New York

First published 1978

Library of Congress Cataloging in Publication Data

Matheson, Ross.
People development in developing countries

"A Halsted Press book."
Bibliography: p.
Includes index.
1. Underdeveloped areas – Manpower policy.
2. Underdeveloped areas – Social conditions.   I. Title.
HD5852.M37   1978   331.1'1   77–28208

ISBN 0 470 99382 0

© Ross Matheson 1978

Typeset by
Computacomp (UK) Limited, Fort William, Scotland
Printed and bound in Great Britain by
Billing & Sons Ltd., Guildford, London and Worcester

Contents

Preface		xiii
Introduction		xv
Chapter 1	*The environment*	1
	Acknowledge the differences	1
	Terminology barriers	2
	Locating the definition of management	2
	Strategy derives from the environment	3
	Respect for a local situation	5
	The national uniqueness syndrome	8
	Conclusion	10
Chapter 2	*The dynamics*	11
	Making new knowledge meaningful	11
	Providing a reality-based context	13
	Making new knowledge motivating	14
	Review of the dynamic processes	15
	Management in terms of process	16
	Management in terms of components	17
	Management in terms of content	21
	Aids to effectiveness	24
	Identification of practical needs	25
	Awareness of and utilisation of resources	28
	Meaningful within a given level of understanding	33
	The key concept	41
	Conclusion	42

Chapter 3 *Practical aids*   45

Implementation against a planned
background   45
    Phase 1 – Language   45
    Phase 2 – Function or skills   46
    Phase 3 – Managing   48
Highly structured and open-ended   51
Further aids to localising   78
For senior staff   80
The demands of reality   87
Conclusion   88

Chapter 4 *Implications*   90

Selection – The basic implication   90
Training – The reality   102
The need to plan – The second
implication   103
    Dynamic organisation charting   104
    Performance assessment   107
    *Individual assessment and development
    planning*   108
    *Inventorisation of individual assessments and
    needs*   109
    Management development planning   110
    Career and succession planning   110
    Pre-planning of personnel strategy   113
    Pre-planning of policy announcements   117

A further reality – Problem-
identification the key Step to structured
solutions   118
    Problem areas to be overcome   120
Implications for countries   122
Aiding government relations   127
    Practical guiding principles   128

The transfer of technology – Through
people 131
Conclusion 135

Chapter 5 *The expatriate question* 137

The need for a deliberate process 137
The facts behind the emotions 138
'There' 141
Consequences for expatriate selection 142
Understanding through empathy 149
Conclusion 150

Chapter 6 *Key points and summarised conclusions* 151

Summarised conclusions and further
inferences 151
Brief advice to the multinationals 156
Local language and culture – The added
value 160
The philosophy at work 165

Appendices:

I 'Understanding' to overcome
isolation 170
II Strategic planning 172
III The staff development and
training committee approach 176
IV Cross-cultural group dynamics –
Fragility, sincerity and self-
control 178
V The mirror-centred approach;
The manager as a professional;
cases for colleagues 181
VI Employee counselling – A training
aid 200
VII The organisation-profile approach
and the self-declaration form 207

VIII More language dimensions   215
IX   Multi-country seminar scenario
      example   216
X   Caution regarding short-term
      expatriate assignments   231
XI   The Ten Commandments for
      travellers   232
XII   Who is judging whom?   234

Reference note   241
Index   243

Illustrations

Figure 1.1	Influencing factors on behaviour	6
Figure 2.1	People development in the context of the business cycle	12
Figure 2.2	The business cycle	17
Figure 2.3	The basic definition	18
Figure 2.4	The basic components	18
Figure 2.5	The unity concept	19
Figure 2.6	The extended components	19
Figure 2.7	Towards accomplishment through the components	19
Figure 2.8	Implications of 'Accomplishment'	20
Figure 2.9	Environmental factors	20
Figure 2.10	The development gap	21
Figure 2.11	Towards accomplishment through the content	22
Figure 2.12	Basic needs analysis	25
Figure 2.13	Task content and completion matrix	26
Figure 2.14	Communications analogue	36
Figure 2.15	Task approach to leadership	39
Table 3.1	Example of the planned three-phase approach	50
Table 3.2	Communicating: pre-reading 1	55
Table 3.3	Communicating: pre-reading 2	56

Table 3.4	Communicating: pre-reading 3	57
Table 3.5	Communicating: pre-reading 4	58
Table 3.6	Communicating: Input 1: Definition	60
Table 3.7	Communicating: Input 2: Dual purpose	61
Table 3.8	Communicating: Discussion guide 1	63
Table 3.9	Communicating: Input 3: Value of keeping people informed	64
Table 3.10	Communicating: Discussion guide 2	65
Table 3.11	Communicating: Input 5: Barriers to effective communications	66
Table 3.12	Communicating: Discussion guide 3	68
Table 3.13	Communicating: Input 6: Making communications effective	69
Table 3.14	Communicating: Discussion guide 4	72
Figure 3.1	Interviewing and counselling: Input 4: The aim of interview conversation	74
Table 3.15	Interviewing and counselling: Input 3: Behaviour	75
Table 3.16	Introductory segment: Input 2: The title 'Manager'	76
Table 3.17	Needs analysis: Sample question and action sheets	84
Table 4.1	The interviewer's basic job knowledge	93
Table 4.2	The interviewer's detailed knowledge	94
Table 4.3	Information to be obtained or confirmed	97
Table 4.4	Interviewing role play I: Standard	99
Table 4.5	Interviewing role play II: Environment related	100

Figure 4.1	Dynamic organisation charting	105
Figure 4.2	Look-ahead chart	106
Table 4.6	Skills, function and knowledge requirements	109
Figure 4.3	Career and succession planning	112
Table 4.7	Management guide outline	118
Figure 6.1	In-country application	157
Figure 6.2	Towards common conceptual understanding	158
Figure 6.3	Increasing effectiveness	160
Figure 6.4	Why training?	161
Figure 6.5	What is effectiveness?	161
Figure 6.6	What is the measurement?	162
Figure 6.7	Dynamic task setting	162
Figure 6.8	Needs Analysis	163
Figure 6.9	Towards planning – exposing the gap	163
Figure 6.10	Towards training	164
Figure 6.11	Closing the gap	164
Figure 6.12	Towards performance	164
Table A.1	Strategic planning check list	172
Table A.2a	Impatience as a virtue	183
Table A.2b	Impatience as one of the criteria in selecting potential managers	183
Table A.2c	One man's philosopy	184
Table A.2d	Sarcasm – expedient for the weak	184
Table A.2e	The nature of criticism	185
Table A.2f	The cynic	185
Table A.2g	Symptoms of the little man	186
Table A.2h	Managerial growth factors	186
Table A.2i	Let yourself go	187
Table A.2j	Help others let go	188
Table A.2k	Your staying power	188

Table A.2l	Wisdom	189
Table A.2m	Habits to be resisted	190
Table A.2n	Self knowledge, the first step to counselling others	191
Table A.3	Sample counselling questionnaire	202
Table A.4	Company profile questionnaire	208
Table A.5	Self declaration form	213
Table A.6	Multi-country seminar scenario	218
Table A.7	*The Ten Commandments for Travellers*	233

Preface

Initiated in 1976, when I was first forced to rethink and restate the experiences of my earlier years by an invitation to speak in Guam to a mixed group of Micronesians and Americans, this book has for the most part been written since that time in aircraft and airport transit lounges.

The content has emerged from countless discussions with people of many nationalities. Many of the basic input ideas result from more than twenty years of reading the works of other authors and, again, countless government publications. In such a book therefore there can never be a claim to total originality and it is hoped that those who may see elements of their own thoughts reflected in this book will feel that fact as a compliment.

The claim that can perhaps be made, and it is in part also the purpose of the book, is that it demonstrates the application of the various management philosophies against a living and dynamic background. The management of change is a well enough known concept, but here the problem is one of appropriate management within a climate of change. The hope is that others will develop the thoughts and further expand understanding in this area.

As a note of both acknowledgement and gratitude it must be mentioned that, while the attitudes, expressed values and practical content of the book have been acquired and developed through personal experience, it is more than coincidental that they also reflect something of the philosophy of my employer. In this regard it has been my good fortune to be employed by Philips, a company that for many years has been among the largest electronics companies in the world and has at the same time retained its international reputation in the field of people management.

It has been said that the inclusion in the title of the words 'developing countries', could be read as being patronising – in fact the book is written as an absolute denial of such a point of view. Being a citizen of a country with an harmonious multiracial society, and with the barest minimum of international influence, it would indeed be difficult to even feel patronising. On the other hand coming from such a country perhaps helps to avoid aggressive nationalism and leaves the mind open, to the thoughts of others.

In writing this preface two thoughts come to mind. One is a memory of having heard from a Samoan gentleman that the greatest difficulty of that island community was its lack of leadership potential, and then later on a Sunday morning, walking through the bush trails and seeing the young men in their sparkling white shirts going from village to village to encourage people to attend the church services. They walked tall, were polite, gently insistent and self-assured – and there were many of them. The other memory is of a not-so-young man, crippled but determined, sitting amid a pile of wood chips in a village which is in part devoted to restoring the craft work of the local culture in the British Solomon Islands. In one hand he held a much cared-for axe and in the other a block of bark-encased hardwood. By looking into the wood the expression on his face clearly showed that he could see the completed carving. At that moment he was a complete man sensing both the vision and his ability to make it a reality. One of his earlier works portraying a number of faces carved in rough detail, but presenting his ideas of several nationalities, he called 'The Family of Life'. Through the good fortune of time and place I was able to buy it – its real value, though, is the invoked memory.

As a final thought, a comment by a friend and colleague in Taiwan. The comment here referred to a forthcoming discussion and there was no doubt who was being counselled: 'Give him a naturally recognised sense of direction and you will capture his interest – persuade him through *his* logic.'

R. MATHESON, Tokyo, February 1978

Introduction

One of the most outstanding economic events of the past twenty years has been the rapid pace of the changes taking place in the emerging countries. The challenge of modifying, changing, and redirecting energies and attitudes is being met. Thoughts and activities are being focused on the future. The role of the management skills in this process of change has been significant and can only become more so in future. Essentially the fact of growth is accomplished by people. It cannot emerge simply through the wishes of a government any more than it can spring from a simple increase in capital investment. It is the result of the development of directed individual effort and enthusiasm and of the most positive utilisation of 'human resources'.

Such growth can only be placed in real perspective when the size of the initial gap between the emerging and the developed countries is appreciated. It was, and in some cases still is, a gap created by historical and environmental circumstance, but any comparison made today has to include an examination of total societies. In a developed or industrialised country society has inbuilt economic norms, patterns of life and expectations that are the result of generations of painstaking deliberate development. It contains an accumulation of knowledge which finds expression not only in its institutions and its patterns of thought, but also in its various disciplines. Expectations are based on previous experiences, discoveries are usually the result of the application of current knowledge, and while life contains its peaks and valleys it also contains its stability and security. In a less developed country it can be the very absence of these things that makes growth difficult. There is less recognition of ability, less thought given to the future, little attention to potential, and in many cases little interest in change.

The challenge, then, is a challenge facing a total society but the instruments for change are the individuals within that society. Whatever political or social path a government may wish to follow and regardless of the political or other events that created the springboard for change, the changes themselves can become reality only if the wishes are actioned through people who are skilled in management or administration. In the longer term it will be the quality of such people which will to a large extent determine the lasting quality of the changes.

Against this background the critical issue is the development of managers or 'management development', but the total span of development is indeed much broader and cannot be defined within narrow or restrictive limits. In this context it becomes a matter of educating, of enthusing, of motivating and of moving people to action. It is in fact a matter of 'people development'. The principles of economic life, of organising and being organised, of working and supervising, of earning and consuming, and of preparing for unknown challenges and demands which have to be passed on to a society. As the future is always with the young people, these become the most potent agents for change.

Effective people development, then, must be a major component of national development. Certainly planning for any form of industrial or other development would be of little consequence without aligned plans for the development of the people who supply the major resource.

In precise terms education in management, education in training and in the whole process of people development must be a vital factor in bringing new realities to the emerging countries. For those countries already well on the road to development and for those at all the various stages of emergence, the need for the rapid development of managers and administrators is fundamental. Inevitably as development takes place the problems are compounded by the speed of developments elsewhere and any shortage of such people will seriously affect the rate and social peace of such growth.

In recognising the joint relationship between national development and the development of managers and administrators any emerging country must therefore ensure that both the present managers and those of the future are equipped with the knowledge, attitudes and skills, the technical, conceptual and human abilities and the philosophy of accomplishment that will enable it to create and maintain its place in a changing world. Within these concepts there are also the essential economic, social and political self disciplines that are themselves subject to the changes that spring from an industrialised environment.

Managers and administrators can only develop over time, the length of that time being determined by both functional demands and the natural abilities. Some will emerge faster than others, but these are the exceptions. This element of time can only be compressed by structured and programmed approaches that are geared to provide understanding of the concepts and philosophies that are themselves directed towards the development of a group, who, in their turn, will be skilled in the development of others.

As 'management' becomes more professional it tends to become knowledge-centred. Recorded successes are generalised into theories so that they can be studied and applied. New theories, new commitments to society, to human dignity and to the human implications of change have developed alongside today's more intensive investigations. All of these forces are also at work within the emerging countries, so that those countries that are now industrialising have also to face many of the same changes that have become familiar in the developed countries. The complexities of collective bargaining and of participative management come in many shades and colours and, while the problems that they bring with them may be different, they are certainly not less difficult.

Added to these situational problems there are others that often have their roots in the fact that while one part of an economy may be aggressively modernising, another part – perhaps the greatest – may still be based on a subsistence economy. In some cases the growth may be built on the foundation of one natural resource, as with copper in

Zambia. At other times, as in the case of many of the South East Asian countries, the only resource may be the potential skills of a large number of people. Other problems relate to industry's responsibility for community development and education. But in all cases, regardless of the nature of the problem, development in one sector of an economy cannot take place in isolation. It brings with it new patterns of living and new expectations from life itself.

Industrialisation and nationalism tend to go hand-in-hand, with either one bringing about the other. Regardless of the order of the events the process itself brings its own problems, particularly for those organisations and institutions that utilise expatriate employees. The natural tendency is for a country to wish to have its own people in positions of responsibility and while this can be an emotion-laden topic it is one that has to be faced. While there is no one solution it is apparent that the planned approach to manpower and management planning that is an integrated part of management development becomes a tool of critical importance. Such problems can only be solved if they are based on staff succession planning and directed training and staff development, together with an equal mixture of common sense and realistic thinking.

In dealing with this topic of people development the work of the so-called multinational companies cannot be neglected. Again this topic has acquired its own emotional overtones and suspicions but reality denies that it can be ignored. While the subject is not given specific attention in the text it is nevertheless an integral part of the total content.

The essential purpose of what follows is to expose and examine the driving forces, to isolate problem areas and to suggest practical solutions. Clearly many functional aspects relate only to the emerging countries, but there are many other aspects that will have direct application to those countries that have matured beyond the standard emerging-country definition and are emerging as dynamic, developed economies.

In all cases the essence of the suggested approaches is that they are both proven and practical and, against this background, the key words within the text could immediately be summarised as 'in context' and 'action-centred'.

1   The environment

Acknowledge the differences

While there is little to be gained from debating the lack of
flexibility contained in the frequently quoted generalisation
that 'the concepts and practices within the process of
managing transcend social and cultural differences', it can
be stated that in teaching and applying the concepts the
social and cultural differences do have to be taken into
account.

Implicit here when comparing emerging countries and
when making the comparison between emerging and
developed countries is a need for honesty in acknowledging
all aspects of these differences. To pretend that they do not
exist is to deny the necessity of differences in the learning
methods that will be essential. To be embarrassed by them –
either as the foreigner looking in, or as the outward-looking
local person – is to close the door to the realities of the
situation. There are differences – just as there are
differences between developed countries and different
stages of development. Generally such differences result
from the centuries that have gone before and in neither
case it is possible for any one man to feel responsible for the
degree of difference. The responsibility is only to resolve the
differences in such a way that the needs, the pride and the
self-respect of all those involved are safeguarded.

Here there is a need for a very basic assumption and that
is that there exists a desire for new learning, new experience
and for change. This is not denying the almost inevitable
unpreparedness for the implications of the change and
subsequent reactions against it. Such an assumption is
important because it helps to make meaningful the fact that

people are prepared to make the initial comparison between 'what is' and 'what could be' – and then to do something about it.

Terminology barriers

Previous experience has provided many examples and lessons regarding misunderstandings of intent through language and of the emotive meaning of words. 'Underdeveloped' and 'developing' can be immediate barriers in creating the impression of the superiority of one group and the inferiority of another. Similarly 'foreigner' and 'local people' can cause the same feeling. The important point here is the manner in which the words are used. If it is condescending or if it is with embarrassment there can be no real communication, and if there is no communication there can be no understanding. What is required is an equal mixture of frankness and sincerity.

The American in America is no more foreign than the Ugandan in Uganda, and the Englishman in London is as much a local person as the Pakistani in Karachi. In none of these cases is there any inbuilt colour, racial or cultural overtone. The words exist only to aid the understanding.

Locating the definition of management

Taking the generally accepted definition, management can be broadly defined as being largely a process of accomplishing predetermined objectives through the efforts of others, the essential point has to be added that accomplishment takes place in a given situation with a given group of people.

If that definition of management seems to ignore the new sophistications it can further be said that the techniques of management have to be made meaningful within a particular environment so that the objectives within that environment can be accomplished.

Here the essential assumption is that an effort is made to understand the significance of all the influencing environmental factors – many of which will have been taken for granted for centuries. This aspect, combined with the desire for change and with a frank and sincere relationship with the agent for change, comprise the initial basic requirements.

Strategy derives from the environment

Whether seen from the point of view of an investing organisation or of a government seeking change, the environmental aspect is fundamental. It is clearly not sufficient only to look at the supply of labour, the water supply or to think only of the stability or strength of the government.[1] Within the terminology of management strategy other fundamental questions will refer to

- the existing and required people skills
- the trends of social and cultural change
- the speed of such trends
- an analysis of likely attitudes to the developments that have been considered, and, in the case of an investing organisation, an analysis of the likely attitudes to the normal characteristic methods and philosophies of the organisation.
- an analysis of the various factors that are normally considered motivating within the environment.
- a resultant analysis of the leadership styles that have proved, or are likely to prove, appropriate.[2]

These are all questions that will later arise as problems if not answered in the early stages. Early and informed answers on the other hand will openly expose the needs, and in terms of the development of people the answers will provide a sense of direction and purpose to the critical development areas. By applying modern interpretive techniques to such an analysis it is clearly possible to

1 See also the brief illustrative notes in Appendix II, p. 172.

2 The application aspect is further explored on p. 137 and in the succeeding pages.

develop a planned approach with a real and informed
chance of success.

The three very practical points here are that in
considering the task of introducing management and staff
development activities into emerging countries, first there
must be an awareness of the social and cultural realities;
second, development of people should be seen as an
accomplishment-oriented investment; and, third, it has to
be appreciated that accomplishment takes place within and
through a local environment. Though self-evident when
stated as basic criteria, these points are often overlooked not
only by organisations and institutions eager to make a
positive contribution, but also by governments wishing to
modernise and develop their existing institutions. The
young man from the New Hebrides Condominium sent to
Fiji to study agriculture for three years who returns to his
village to find not only a complete lack of interest, but also
an absence of both fertilisers and tractors is an obviously
frustrated man. But, so too is the man who is sent from Dar-
es-Salaam to Dallas to acquire the skills of marketing, and
the local company manager in Afghanistan who invests in
an American-style packaged motivation programme –
complete with sound track! It is just not that simple.

Other points relating to the environment help to make
clear the difference between the developed and the
emerging countries. Even taking into account those
exceptions of the organisations in the developed countries
that are managed on a paternal and sometimes seemingly
'tribal' basis, and, likewise, those companies in the
emerging countries that are up-to-date as the latest
textbook, the essence of the difference remains. In the
emerging country such an organisation is often operating
in isolation and its greatest difficulty can be that it is out of
step with the surrounding environmental infrastructure.
There is often an absence of an unified sense of direction,
no experience base, very little on-tap information and in
many cases an alarming lack of predictability.

In these days of 'go' and 'no go' definitions it is normal to
define the environmental factors under the heading of
constraints and opportunities and to examine them under
the familiar categories of social, cultural, economic and

political. Essentially the factor being analysed is one of 'current capability'. Such a measurement could be depressing unless it is placed in the context of finding out 'where we are now' because 'we want to know the steps that we have to take to get to where we want to go'. The results can then be seen in terms of potential capability which make them highly action-centred and motivating.

The one certain point in an emerging country is that changes in the infrastructural environment will occur at a faster pace than in a developed country. Other related certainties are that the period of such change will be a trial of nerves, of strength, of patience and of tolerance to frustrations and delay. These at least are predictable.[3]

Respect for local situation

A further essential point in the context of people development is understanding, or making an effort to understand, the behaviour of a local people and the patterns of local life. Here there is no implication of adopting a superior attitude. It is totally a matter of respecting a local situation. Further, one of the major studies within any country contemplating any form of industrial development must be to come to terms with the effects of that industrialisation on the pattern of life of the people most effected. Once change takes place in this area it creates change in every other area of daily life and people's expectations from life are subject to change.

It will be clear that 'all' people have to be seen:
- within their culture
- within the context of their opportunities for, attitude to and ultimate use of education
- within the limits of the development of their depth and flexibility of thinking and their capacity to exercise initiative
- against the background of their actual work history and their attitudes to work itself.

The well-known behavioural theories and illustrations are an aid to thinking and in this regard in looking for a

---

3 This aspect is further developed on pp. 121, 124 and 129.

ready frame of reference it will be useful to consider the content of Figure 1.1, 'Influencing factors on behaviour'.[4]

Figure 1.1   Influencing factors on behaviour[5]

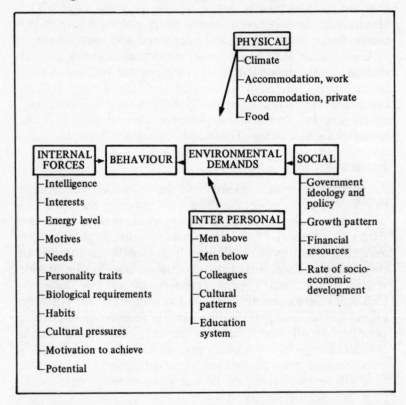

The content of this chart has been derived from practical experience in several countries. It is provided only as an aid to thinking and the answers derived from the chart in different countries could lead to many different solutions. This presentation has the advantage of separating the three factors of the physical, the interpersonal and the internal influences and this in itself makes it clear that far from

4 For acknowledgement of this material please see the Reference note, p. 241.

5 Further elaboration regarding practical behavioural theory is provided on p. 75.

being theoretical this relatively simple chart can direct attention to some far-reaching and practical points.

In terms of the physical influences it is not uncommon for all people living within X degrees of the equator to be labelled as lazy – the exact number of degrees being apparently determined by where the generaliser has his own roots.

Also under this heading it is useful to consider the standard of usual private accommodation – not in order to minimise the conditions projected for a factory or an office but at least to be aware of the significance of the projected differences.

Interpersonal influences can be profound and, to those not able to anticipate events, can be at the very least disturbing. In many sectors of the underdeveloped emerging world, absenteeism can be a great frustration, but again understanding of cultural patterns and cultural demands can avoid the unexpected. Here as in most other cases the first step is to examine local practice and, if, for example, it is local practice to provide four days' leave for a funeral, perhaps it is reasonable initially not to diverge too much from the custom. Similarly if it is tribal practice that the prince is the natural supervisor perhaps it is best to first make an effort to employ and develop a local prince.

A foreign building contractor in a particular South Pacific Island learned these lessons many years ago. For several years the Company tried the traditional methods of developing supervisory staff. They selected the best tradesmen and sent them to standard supervisory courses in the home country. Any success was short-lived and after the first of two occasions when the death of a relative was the occasion for a prolonged feast, the newly promoted supervisors were as reluctant to return to work as they had ever been. Fate eventually provided the solution when a local prince proved also to be a good tradesman and the discipline that resulted was as natural as the necessity to conform to local custom. Fortunately for the contractor each tribe had several princes and he was wise enough to recognise the solution.

Far from being facetious these are points of realism, all of which can be readily formalised. First look at local practice, then look at the local legal requirements, consider accepted company practice, discuss, decide and inform. In terms of people development the actions indicated are significant indications of the realisation that adaptation is multidirectioned and mutual. The point is not made to indicate that local practice should be decisive but to indicate that it is a factor to be kept in mind when formulating what the intended company practice will be.[6]

The internal influences on behaviour are largely self-explanatory but in this area also it is important to demonstrate the effort to understand. Here example can be drawn from the conduct of two recent managerial seminars. Both were regional, one being in Kenya for the participants of several African countries, the other in Manila for the participants of several Asian countries. In both cases it was necessary to create a rapid seminar identity that would serve to minimise the national differences. Fortunately the short-sleeved and elegant Philippino shirts proved as popular as the loose-fitting shirts available in Kenya. In both cases the instrument was local, with the host country appreciating the courtesy.[7]

The national uniqueness syndrome

A separate point, but one that has to be raised and treated as frankly as the earlier points, relates to the imagined and often self-imposed barrier of national uniqueness. It comes in several forms, which vary from

- 'We are different.'
- 'We are more advanced. Look at our history.'
- 'But they are Asian – African – Indian – Arabs – etc. – etc.'

to
- 'If you knew more about our culture you wouldn't even consider making the comparison.'

---

6 This point is further illustrated on p. 20.

7 A scenario for such occasions is provided in Appendix IX, p. 217.

- 'We have our own ways, our own methods and we will use these to seek change as we have done in the past.'

All true enough, but each one, creating a 'pride barrier' that is extremely difficult to overcome. Not that this is unique to the emerging countries. How often is it said today in Europe 'I doubt that it will work. Isn't it really an American idea?'

Certainly there are differences between peoples and between cultures that extend way beyond colour, craft and language. Certainly also such differences, as has been said earlier, are to be respected and, during times of industrial advancement, a real effort should be made to preserve many of the ways and particularly the craft skills of the past.

But, once the decision to seek change has been expressed, there has to be a period when efforts are directed towards finding the common denominators between countries. This search for the similarities and the finding of points of relevance and of parallels between countries will produce an ever-increasing number of clearly recognisable points of common interest in terms of both needs and solutions. 'Cross-cultural applicability' is rather a grand term but it does serve as an overall heading to describe the feasibility of the application of systems, procedures, policies and practices, both internationally and across cultures.[8]

The experiences in one country can be useful inputs for the problems of another country – particularly for another country that is in a similar stage of development. The differences between those countries will then be concerned with matters of application – either in terms of the speed of implementation or of the actual mechanics of applying a given principle.

The alternative to what is suggested here is a constant reinvention of the wheel – costly, time-consuming and non-productive.

---

8 Cross-cultural applicability is given further emphasis on p. 29 and is illustrated on p. 157.

Conclusion

● People development is an accomplishment-oriented investment. The fact that it is very often at best a medium-term investment is of fundamental importance when it is seen alongside the more short-term aspects of the associated investments. Rather than being regarded as a disincentive this medium- and longer-term consideration must be seen as being complementary to the whole process of change.

● The critical factor in developing people in emerging countries is to have precise information regarding all factors in the environemnt. This requires a wide field of studies ranging through the behaviour patterns of people to the basic elements of the infrastructure.

● Undoubtedly it will be found that all countries are different and just as undoubtedly it will be found that among these differences there are many similarities.

● Particularly it will be found that there are similarites in terms of the nature of the problems to be solved.

● This also leads to the discovery that there are similarities in the solutions to the problems. The shades of difference that emerge can to a great extent be resolved by differences in the application of the solutions. It is here that knowledge of the environmental factors is fundamental.

● It would therefore be valid to suggest that 'Subject to differences in application, the concepts and practices within the process of management can be attuned to various social and cultural environments'.

2 The dynamics

Another critical difference between the emerging and the developed countries is that theory for its own sake is both less interesting and less useful. What is required is something that is meaningful and can be communicated as being achievable.

Here it is necessary to introduce a total conceptual approach which embraces the various tested patterns of management thinking and adds the further element of flexible application that was described in Chapter 1.

An outline of this conceptual approach is provided in Figure 2.1.

Making new knowledge meaningful

At this point it is necessary to introduce a further word which, if misunderstood, could create another terminology barrier. As is the case of the words mentioned earlier, the term 'desophistication' carries with it its own emotive overtone and all possible reasons for total mis-understanding.

As has been proven many times one of the vital skills in promoting learning is the ability to strip new knowledge of its unnecessary sophistications. Simply stated, this is the ability to make new and appropriate knowledge meaningful and to ensure understanding within a given set of personal relationships. An alternative expression could be to use the words 'optimum sophistication' but while they are perhaps more polite they lack the teeth that are necessary to face the realities of what can be a major obstacle to an otherwise well-intentioned learning process.

Figure 2.1   People development in the context of the business cycle

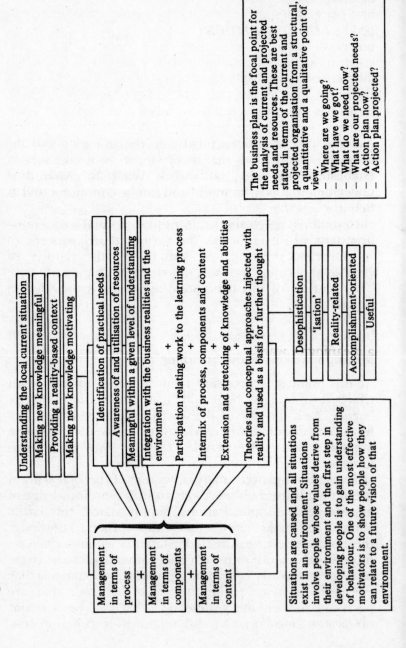

The point has to be made that the knowledge can only be desophisticated if there is real depth of knowledge in the first place. Those who pretend knowledge, like those who peddle closed courses and those who have the ready universal answers, too easily ignore the facts of the environmental differences and the resultant need for differences in the application of solutions.[1]

Critical here is the fact that 'desophisticated' in these terms has no relationship with 'unsophisticated' and none whatever with the prevalence of readily available simplified material. It is a deliberate process of making learning useful in such a way that the formulation of knowledge is established so that both new learning and new understanding can be added. Such an approach ensures that the intelligence of people is respected and further encourages belief in the fact that individual capacities can be expanded.

Counselling in terms of people development in an emerging country is a related skill requiring similar abilities. Clearly, personal training or coaching of an individual may well fail not because of the quality of the input, not because of the attitude of the man seeking new knowledge, but because of his manager's inability to convey the learning in a meaningful way.

Providing a reality-based context

In outline the headlines described in Figure 2.1 provide a familiar presentation – that is, the initial requirement for an analysis of needs and resources and an underlining referring to accomplishment and usefulness.

For people development in emerging countries, however, experience shows that there are several differences in both content and emphasis. Just as there is a uniqueness about the 'local current situation' in terms of environment, so there is a 'process of management' which is part of the uniqueness of each institution or organisation. A basic skill

---

1 The application aspects of this concept are further developed on pp. 133 and 144.

is to use this uniqueness (not abuse it) and to build upon it to provide identity. To a person not exposed to, and probably not easily satisfied by an out-of-context examination of some one piece of management learning or philosophy, the feeling of identity arising from shared uniqueness can be the focal point and talking point of learning. Further:

- There is no mystery about something which is relevant and can be seen to be either a living problem or as an in-context solution.
- There can be a ready acceptance of a tool or technique that aids execution of a function or that makes it easier or faster or in any way visibly more efficient.
- Involvement can be more readily induced if what is said to be useful can at the same time be seen to be useful.
- The desire to achieve or accomplish can grow from a learning situation which derives from the living facts of the daily environment.

Making new knowledge motivating

Another characteristic and in many cases one of the outstanding features of an emerging country can be simple pride – in most cases pride from the heart that is neither comparative nor competitive and even without emphasis on uniqueness. It can be both a revelation and a lesson to hear people reveal their pride of country. It is clear that the man from oil-rich Nigeria will have a dynamic and aggressive interest in learning. His experience makes him familiar with the meaning of applied knowledge. But his pride, and therefore the means of tapping his motivation, is not necessarily greater than that of the man from another African country who has gained what to him is a new-found identity – perhaps through a process of violence or perhaps through a change of flag or country name. It is in this case a matter of what comes next. Pride needs to be supported by reasons to remain proud – reasons that are viable, reasons that are built on growth, understanding, self-respect and respect for others. Here Singapore is an outstanding example. There are few people in the world more proud than the Singaporean – whether of Chinese, Malay or Indian origin. To be Singaporean is to be proud.

This is another side of the coin of nationalism and it is a side that is highly relevant in the field of people development. Giving people a future vision of their environment, of themselves in relation to that changed environment, can be perhaps the most effective medium for making the changes possible:

- A meaningful achievable vision of what the future can become can be one of the most effective motivators for learning.

The door can be opened for the introduction of change in the form of new methods and technologies.

- Revised standards for both behaviour and performance can be revealed at the earliest possible stage.
- That which can be understood to be taking place within the context of familiar surroundings can be believable, achievable and can be made into a reality.

It is through this integration of vision that both the learning process and the change process can be made meaningful.[2]

Review of the dynamic processes

In order further to examine this conceptual aspect of the dynamics it is necessary to look within the content of Figure 2.1 on p. 12.

Many of the concepts presented here are as old as Aristotle – others are as recent as the latest textbook – but, here it is the development mix that is important rather than the theoretical mix. As has been indicated the essential concern is to present knowledge within the broad conceptual framework of people development in such a way that it is meaningful, in context, and motivating.

Let us now examine the three central points of Figure 2.1 in turn.

---

2 This fundamental aspect is viewed in other contexts on pp. 34, 134 and 146.

1 Management in terms of process

In conceptualising rather than theorising under this heading it is possible to satisfy the three criteria.

In any happening there is a process – that process may have developed through tradition or through environmental circumstance, but by countless repetitions the process has become established.

In this regard it is interesting to travel around the world following the same geographical zone. Here the feature that emerges is that the climate has imposed its own disciplines in terms of housing requirements, and, indeed, in so far as there are similarities in the afforestation, on the whole pattern of architecture and design. This physical manifestation can also be seen in the methods of fishing, planting rice, wood-carving and so on. Within each island group or land mass there are differences – so much so that the comparison of any two would hardly reveal the similarities.

This aspect of process exists in a context and when it is revealed within that context the chain of events that forms it can be shown to have pattern and design. This range of processes will vary through the total range of daily activities including those mentioned above, but will also extend to some other activities such as the centuries-old navigation maps found in the Micronesian Islands. These indications of tides, reefs and winds made possible massive migrations of people using techniques that today are still being studied. The point here is that these environment-centred activities can be as varied in complexity as the more measured events of a modern industrial society.

The act of charting these familiar processes will be effective in illustrating the fact that such descriptive diagrams can reveal new ways of teaching and at the same time provide for recognition of possible changes in the process itself.

Presented in such a way the concept of process becomes meaningful, can be related to the normal business cycle, and can be set out diagramatically as in Figure 2.2.

The interesting point about such a presentation is that it can be used both 'backwards' and 'forwards'. That is, it can

Figure 2.2   The business cycle

Taking	Goal-setting
corrective action	Criteria-selection
or	Planning and organisation
seeking process	Executing or directing
improvement	Controlling results

be a vehicle for describing a traditional process and at the same time it can be developed as a means of illustrating something as complex as the whole process of budgeting – one of the most fundamental and at the same time one of the most difficult concepts of modern management. The fact that an approach of this kind can provide such an easy bridge between the past and the present makes it inherently motivating.

A further point here is that the concept of 'management in terms of process' can be used in countries at any stage of development. In the more advanced of the emerging countries there are many examples of institutions and organisations which have developed their own processes of management and discovered the fact that the detail within the process will contain individual differences and points of uniqueness.

Here also it is fundamental to recognise that a particular process of management will be a reflection of the attitudes and principles of a particular organisation. If that organisation operates in a number of countries it will emerge that each separate environment will exert its own, sometimes subtle, influence on that process.

2 Management in terms of components

In this case it is a matter of presenting a theoretical concept so that it can be seen as living, dynamic and important as an aid to meaningful understanding.

Just as there is no one perfect all-embracing theory of the basic management principles, so there is no one way to make such a presentation. At the same time it can be shown that when packaged concisely the theories can be sufficiently summarised to include the real essentials and avoid the confusion that can arise from presenting a too-complex initial picture.

With this as a guideline the least confusing and the most convincing method of presentation is perhaps to commence with the most basic definition and with the 'unity concept' of what management is. Such an approach is exampled in the sequence of boxed diagrams that follows.

Figure 2.3   The basic definition

Management is concerned with accomplishing predetermined results with and through the efforts of others.

First the definition, as set out in Figure 2.3. This can be broken down for discussion into the basic components set out in Figure 2.4.

Figure 2.4   The basic components

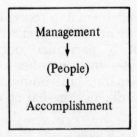

In turn such an approach readily promotes discussion of the 'getting things done' principle, which can be used as a lead in to the fact that, while the single word 'management' is intended to convey a total approach embracing all facets of organisation and execution (see Figure 2.5), it is both practical and useful to look into its component parts. Here

Figure 2.5   The unity concept

```
Management

is a unity concept

but ——
```

the components used may vary but, to continue with the 'traditional' illustrations, they could be presented as in Figure 2.6.

Figure 2.6   The extended components

```
Components—
    Planning
    Organising
    Controlling
    Co-ordinating
    Motivating
```

Clearly the scope for discussion at this point can be extended in the direction of any of the key words. But to continue the illustration at a basic but sound discussion level the optimum approach could be to return to the definition and to restate it as in Figure 2.7.

Figure 2.7 Towards accomplishment through the components

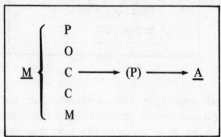

At this point of the presentation it will be clear that the intention of creating a feeling of living dynamism around a definition can be accomplished.

Figure 2.8   Implications of 'accomplishment'

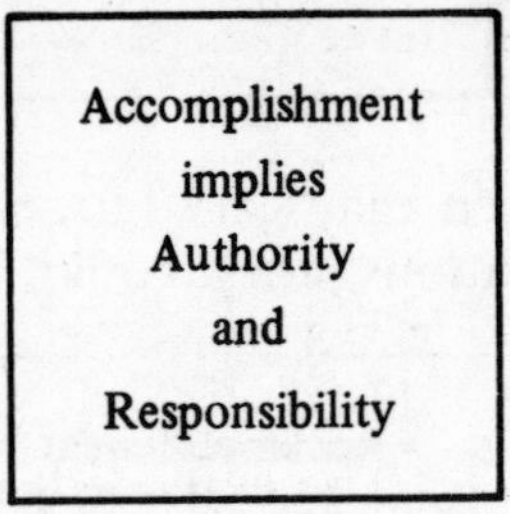

Accomplishment
implies
Authority
and
Responsibility

There is in fact no limit to this introductory approach, but to continue only with the key word 'accomplishment' it is possible to lead into the implications of the word (see Figure 2.8), or, to fit the term into the environment, as in Figure 2.9, and look into the various aspects that have to be kept in mind before what seems like a good idea is finally introduced.

Figure 2.9   Environmental factors

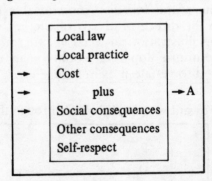

Local law
Local practice
Cost
        plus
Social consequences
Other consequences
Self-respect

→A

As a final example to illustrate the significance of maintaining a key word, promoting a feeling of familiarity with it and using it as a core concept, it is possible to take one of the most familiar and effective of the AMA[3] illustrations and by changing one word produce the development gap illustrated in Figure 2.10. Again the three criteria of 'meaningful, in context, and motivating' can be readily satisfied. Utilising the basic concept allows for ease of comparison with local situations and any group task at any stage of traditional development can be accommodated within the illustrations.

Figure 2.10   The development gap

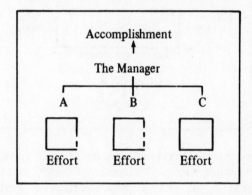

3 Management in terms of content

Here the style and depth of explanation depends for a large part on the circumstance of any particular institution or company.

Ideally, when dealing with specific examples, it is a matter of exposing organisation theory by practical reference to the various organisation segments such as marketing, finance and accounting, and adding explanations of the most significant of the appropriate support functions. Unfortunately, the usefulness of generalisations, in relation to these topics, even as discussion backdrops, is questionable; but there are other approaches which may be used to give shape and a sense of vision to the total subject.

---

3 Amended from the original American Management Association Basics of Management programme and utilised in this context through the courtesy of Dean J. Hayes. Please also see p. 241.

By analysing 'management' and its relationship with accomplishment, the functions of government or institutional and organisation management can be presented in diagrammatic form, as in Figure 2.11.

Figure 2.11 Towards accomplishment through the content

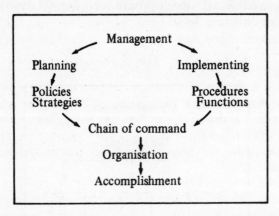

Organisation is then seen as a means of implementation and, when made more effective and efficient, would tend to be a greater aid to a more efficient and effective implementation. This approach has the advantage of immediately placing the concept of organisation in its true perspective as being derived from the purpose and goals rather than as an imposed set of restrictive constraints.

A natural growth sequencing under the heading of organisation is readily available in the emerging country context by reference to the one-man organisation, the father and son organisation, the father and two sons, and so on. This in itself can be completely in context and totally motivating. Comparison with major growth companies that started from such beginnings are abundantly available. It is also only a short step from such an illustration to proceed to the various aspects of functional organisation.

One often neglected element of major importance is the role of organisation as a tool in shaping the future. Here the aspect of vision becomes paramount. A picture of 'what can be' can be drawn with all its component parts and in all its various stages of growth. The so called 'look-ahead chart' when used in this context takes on a new significance and can be a vital tool for short-, medium- and long-term planning.[4]

A further significant point is that the emerging countries that adopt these approaches can take advantage of the progress that has occurred in their developed counterparts. For example, in the field of task-setting and standards of performance such tools can be used at the outset of development. They can be built into the visionary aspect, become standard practices and so avoid many years of costly 'growing pains'. Of course there can and will be resistance to some of these developments simply because they are American, or European, or British, or whatever, but the point is that if the techniques are at least considered in the earliest possible stages, each country in applying them can add its own particular traditional style or emphasis.

As stated, it is not the intention to examine the content of the various 'functions' of management. This is best seen as an in-company or in-institution activity and any company or institution will need to make its own in-depth analysis of these aspects. However there are some key points to be kept in mind:

- First establish the purpose of the enterprise and organise to achieve that purpose.
- If it is true that the resources available are men, money and materials then it is equally true that the organisation will require human, financial and technical segments.
- Neither men nor machines can go on for ever without service but in both cases it has to be organised for and planned.
- If the purpose of the business is to sell, whether it be a product or a service, the object will probably be to increase both the quality and the quantity of the sales. Concern about growth will therefore be a major feature of the organisation.
- Items such as span of control can be eliminated as

---

4 An example of this tool is provided on p. 106.

major issues if they are never allowed to develop into minor problems.

- An organisation has to be staffed but it is nevertheless perfectly normal to have a position to be filled listed as a vacancy until such time as someone is shown to be fully competent to fill that position.
- The writing down of the chain of command imposes a commitment to maintain and enforce it.
- Used effectively the title manager should carry with it the ability to manage.
- Key questions to incorporate in organisation planning from a position point of view are
  (i)   What is the purpose of this function?
  (ii) What are the human requirements of this function in priority order?
  (iii) What are the job requirements of this function in priority order?
  (iv) What exactly, in order of importance, is the holder of this position accountable for and to whom?
- Boxes imposing limits on initiative cannot be motivating. Clear definitions of the area of responsibility can be.

Aids to effectiveness

Given that the most basic starting point is to 'know where we are going' and given the fact that finding the answer implies a thorough knowledge of the environmental circumstances; given also the need to place knowledge in context, to make it meaningful and motivating; given an insight into the process, the components and the content of management – the responsibility remains to build on the vision and to create a new reality.

Many practical means of completing this task will be explained in Chapter 3 but first there are several back-up support concepts to be explored.[5]

---

5 These themes are further developed on pp. 82–6 and 102–13.

1 Identification of practical needs

As is stated in Figure 2.1 on p. 12, in analysing the current and projected needs, 'these are best stated in terms of the current and projected organisation from a structural, a quantitative and a qualitative point of view.'

Figure 2.12   Basic needs analysis

Where are we going?

What have we got?

What do we need now?

What are our projected needs?

Action plan now?

Action plan projected?

When we explore this concept, as in Figure 2.12, we see that it is a matter of being totally realistic when combining the elements of knowledge, skills and attitudes, and seeing the practical possibilities for growth over a specific time scale.

From the previously acquired environmental knowledge the essential elements will be clear:

- The education structure, content, and level will be known.[6]
- The skill content will be on display. In the most basic cases it will be possible through the various survival and craft skills to recognise the areas for potential development. In the more developed cases there will be examples of the use of applied skills within the already changing economy.
- The attitudes to education, to learning in general, and to the acquiring of particular physical or mental dexterities will have been studied as an essential element of the infrastructure.

---

6 See also p. 5 and for further implications pp. 101 and 121.

In terms of time, however, the problem is one of knowing the precise requirements over the various stages of projected growth. It is in fact this element which is fundamental, as both the 'action plan now' and the 'action plan projected' are dependent, in the final analysis, on the accuracy and subsequent consistency of the answer to the question 'What is required and when?' Only in those cases where such knowledge is detailed and complete can the actual environmental factors themselves be legitimately blamed for any later failure.

In this regard – as in so many others – the emerging countries have the advantage of having a wealth of experience to draw upon, and again, by avoiding unnecessary sophistications, there are many appropriate devices available.

Figure 2.13   Task content and completion matrix

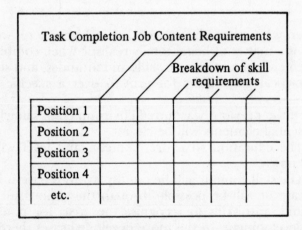

From a structural point of view the most basic matrix is an analysis of skill requirements and job content schedules, as set out in Figure 2.13.

Such an analysis is clearly intended to take place one step ahead of the more familiar training needs matrix which simply analyses skill requirements against existing people. The advantage of the chartered approach will be apparent as it lays the foundation for certain important specific mental disciplines:

- thinking in total task terms
- thinking in terms of task groups
- thinking of job design in terms of total task
- thinking, in addition, of both recruitment and job training requirements as one step; therefore, highlighting performance potential as one of the priorities of recruitment.
- thinking in terms of the several types and levels of skill that are required to perform a total task.

In other words the emphasis in an emerging country can in many cases be more advanced at the outset than is usually the case in the more developed countries. It is clearly a matter of careful selection of approaches so that those that contain the broadest orientation towards self-discipline and the development of appropriate routines, are chosen.

The same figure can be the initial focal point for the qualitative and quantitative analysis. Here again the aspect of time has to be taken into account in terms of:

- The number of people required to be employed when?
- The number with specific qualifications to be employed when?
- The training time for each specific skill?
- The scheduled time requirement for effective on-the-job operation?

The matrix combinations here can be made to suit the particular organisation circumstances and a further point of interest is that, with only minor modifications, the approach can be adapted for a wide-ranging variety of knowledge and skill levels.

In those cases where the analysis of needs is taking place in a semi-developed organisation, the problems will be very little different from those that exist in most developed countries. Certainly to restructure or to retrain is a more difficult process. Again, though, the solution to the problem is to be found in the degree of depth, and accuracy, of the requirements input. At every level the question remains 'What knowledge, what skills, what attitudes, have to be developed?' If there has been *ad hoc* development in the early unstructured stages of growth it must be recognised for what it is. The longer such a situation continues the more difficult it will be to repair. Here again the emerging countries have a clear responsibility to be honest with themselves. Inadequacies created in the early stages can be corrected only be careful analysis of the real needs.

Similarly the most appropriate and effective allocation of resources can only be made possible by the most thorough analysis of the needs. Further particular points of relevance for the emerging country situation are that:

- Knowledge of the needs should be sufficiently penetrating to take into account all aspects of the environment and of the local aspects of behaviour.
- Alongside the pattern of practical needs in terms of training there will also be an emerging pattern of needs in terms of support system, procedures, regulations, disciplines and all of those aspects surrounding the whole process of management.
- In this way the analysis of needs will extend into every phase of organisation.
- The need for knowledge, the need for skills and the need for the encouragement of a set of attitudes will become more specific over a period of time so that growth will impose new needs. Plans for continued growth will therefore depend for a large part on the continued effectiveness of the analysis of needs. Clearly, it is not a one-time process.
- It is fundamental to recognise the fact that training needs, like all other needs, exist not for their own sake but in the context of the purpose of the organisation or business. This should always be the context in which these on-going developments are considered and explored.

This network relationship of the various factors under the heading of needs analysis is typical of the total in-context aspect of the whole concept of people development.

2 Awareness of and utilisation of resources

The essence of this very practical section has already been touched on in Chapter 1 under the heading of 'National uniqueness syndrome'. The main points arising under that heading referred to the facts that

- the search for similarities and the finding of points of relevance and of parallels between countries will produce an increasing number of clearly recognisable points of common interest in terms of both needs and solutions;
- though the needs require to be explored on an in-depth per country basis, the results in one country will be in many aspects to similar to those in another country at the same or similar stage of development;
- this emergence of common denominators will include in particular such aspects as

    systems
    procedures
    policies
    approaches

and it will be found that the experiences in one country can be useful inputs for the problems of another country;
- the term 'cross cultural applicability' is concerned with the feasibility of application and as such is one of the most vital concepts in the rapid emergence of the developing countries.

In those cases where there has been a breaking down of the barriers of national uniqueness, where there has been recognition of the common denominators, and where opportunities have been taken to use proven resources and to share whatever resources are available, the result is invariably the development of a climate of mutual support and learning. This is usually accompanied by a general willingness to 'try it', which in turn through a process of 'isation' can create something peculiarly local out of something which had been initially developed elsewhere. Clearly the outstanding example in this field is Japan.

Few countries have a stronger set of in-built cultural patterns of behaviour, but on the other hand it is probably true that no other country has ever evidenced such a continuing interest in the philosophies and practices of the process and content of management that exist in other countries. In looking at these techniques and tools for managing, the Japanese are able to find those that may have practical significance. These are then studied, digested, and re-born as something entirely Japanese. This Japanisation aspect is one of the ultimate evidences of the value of thinking in terms of application. It implies total awareness and is in no way related to simple copying or to the equally simple purchase of packaged solutions.

Again the practical elements concerning this subject will be found in Chapter 3 but, under the general label of 'back-up support concepts', several initial approaches that have been tried and proven to be effective can be described. For the sake of general interest the few approaches that are summarised here are taken from the whole spectrum of people development and include the elements of skill training, management development and development in terms of directed education:

- *The springboard approach* (residential meetings with those managers already employed)

   useful to explain new directions and revised strategy, plans and specific goals, to indicate clear responsibility areas in terms of people development, to check knowledge of the environment and to gain feed-back information on the results of the change processes;

   as a vehicle for raising suggestions is the ideal aid to commitment;

   provides a channel for both input and output information, which can be readily stimulated.

- *The job description approach* (either through group examination of existing or suggested descriptions, or through the process of the formulation of such a description)

   useful to gain recognition of the various essential inputs for satisfactory job performance, to gain clear understanding of the concept of output – as source material for the construction of job-centred training courses which for the sake of both completeness and simplicity can be headlined by each of the components contained in the job description – provides commitment to an agreed group goal, and provides a local solution which can be based on any available thought starting inputs.

- *The staff development and training committee approach*[7] (creating involvement and a channel for commitment by the appointment of a sub-group of managers)

    can serve as a discussion filter of input data available from other sources, can focus on priorities, can be a means of promoting enthusiasm by association and can in itself be a medium for development.

- *The consultation approach* (individual meetings with a pre-selected level of existing managers or according to some other pre-selected uniform and clearly apparent criteria)

    directed towards gaining individual opinions regarding both needs and solutions;

    can be broadened to any required spread so that individual opinions can be obtained regarding personal progress, group progress and organisation progress;

    in seeking opinions on a personal basis provides maximum recognition and is the ultimate compliment.

- *The organisation profile approach*[8] (employing one of the profile-charting approaches or by adaptation of one of the organisation climate approaches to gain a collective input of opinions and feelings from any one standard level group)

    does involve sound leadership and discussion skills but is particularly useful to create a feeling of solution orientation as opposed to problem orientation.

- *The personal profile approach*:

    similar to the standard approach to appraisal and task setting but structured towards guided self-development and exposure to resources that are individually available.

- *The concept repetition approach* (gaining initial concept acceptance through repetition and reinforcement

---

7 See also the detailed notes for guidance in Appendix III, p. 176.

8 See also the examples provided in Appendix VII, p. 207.

preferably in 'non-teaching' and 'non-classroom' situation)

can be best accomplished by using every reasonable opportunity during individual or group meetings; an essential tool for creating a rapid and recognisable in-house language and sub-culture.

Examples here are:

the concept of management as taking place in a changing or dynamic situation

the concept of effectiveness as being dependent on the appropriate managing of a changing situation

the concept of accomplishment as being the result of 'doing' something effective

the concept of 'result-related' as being a critical component in the process of knowing where you are going

the concept of 'output-related' as contrasted with input-related

the concept of counselling[9] coaching, and task-setting being normal aspects of daily work

the concept of the assessment of others as always taking place against a set of circumstances

the concept of self-awareness and self-knowledge as being critical factors in self-development[10]

the concept of mutual support within and between groups.

These support concepts themselves contain certain common features and among these are:

- the utilisation of every possible occasion for idea injection
- the provision of the maximum number of opportunities to review and localise thinking from other sources
- the promotion of a feeling of involvement and result commitment

---

9 See also the training aid provided in Appendix VI, p. 200.

10 See also the exampled training aids designed for this purpose, in Appendix V, p. 181.

- the continued reinforcement of the concept of promoting suggestions
- the filtering of ideas from any source through a responsible local group with a consequent increase in acceptance
- the use of both idea inputs and outputs to achieve the maximum possible feed-back

Apart from these conceptual approaches there are certain standard steps that are implied within the topic of resource sharing. The first responsibility is of course to discover for each of the revealed need areas a full and comprehensive list of the appropriate resource materials. While the resources within an emerging country may not be immediately apparent it is nevertheless true that in almost all countries there are scholarship systems, government-sponsored visits abroad, visiting professors, military establishments, etc. – all of them avenues which can be explored.

In keeping with the theme of cross-cultural applicability it is also essential to consider the possibilities in any neighbouring country or in similar countries. In fact it will usually be found that there is an abundance of resource material, but to return to the central issue the vital factor is to be precise when defining the needs and to be skilful in applying the resource inputs.

3 Meaningful within a given level of understanding

One of the most easily neglected points is that the management and administrative 'language' that is familiar to a very well-educated minority in an emerging country may be completely unfamiliar to the vast majority of people.[11] This point applies equally to an expatriate group in a similar country and here there may well be the added problem of in-company jargon that often either substitutes for, or complements, the formal management language.

---

11 The concept of 'management language', while being an underlying theme, is given successively greater significance on pp. 40, 45, 50, 115, 117 and pp. 157–64.

The greatest danger in any of these situations is the tendency to assume a level of knowledge that does not in fact exist.

The result of making such assumptions will be to embarrass, to create learning barriers and to invite resistance – to say nothing of the wasted time. Again only a careful pre-study of the environment will reveal the actual level of understanding.

Not only is it critical to know the existing level of understanding, it is also fundamental, in terms of needs, to know both the level of those needs and the level of the thought processes necessary to resolve them. In this regard it could reasonably be expected that there will be an initial need for concentration on basics such as self-discipline, learning to learn, learning to pass on knowledge, and generally a need to build a foundation of knowledge and thinking capacities that will later be able to absorb more specialised inputs.

'Meaningful' in this context also relates to being realistic when structuring a set of norms. There is, for example, little to gain by using job-profile norms that are based on the circumstances in some advanced environment. If the objective is to develop people who can be effective in a demanding and developing local situation, with all its limitations, there is little point in preparing them for a situation which revolves around and tends to rely on computer models and intellectual discussion. What are interesting are the norms that will provide specifications for locally effective administrators, technicians, sales and service staff, etc.

In looking at the experiences of the industrialised countries those that are in the process of development have the opportunity to avoid many of the pitfalls that normally come while acquiring experience. Among these in this context are recognition of the need

- to focus training and development in terms of recognisable needs and goals;
- to reiterate and demonstrate that while management can be discussed under the heading of its components it is practised as a process;

- to be totally conscious of both the realities and the priorities in any situation;
- to maintain an element of entrepreneurial thinking.

Alongside these facts there has to be the added element of growth. In ensuring understanding and in making new learning meaningful, integrating the vision with the reality is both logical and appropriate. People can see themselves in the context of the vision and as being part of the process of its fulfilment; they can see and acknowledge the learning gap; they can see and, to their satisfaction, feel it being closed. These are the living symptoms of growth that make new goals and new efforts possible.

This integration of vision also has to be seen together with the more familiar concept of the integration of interest – that is, the identity of the individual's interest with that of the organisation.[12]

These concepts are not sophisticated but neither are they simple. In themselves they call for a view of reality which embraces the present, the future, the individuals and the various groups. They focus on change and growth and are therefore dynamic. They focus on people and organisation and are therefore alive.

Returning again to the subject of language it is important to reflect on some of the key words contained in the language of management. It is an unfortunate fact that in many of the developed industrialised and sophisticated countries a term like 'communications' has gone through the fashionable stage, has tended to be overused and to a large extent, in having been taken for granted, has lost much of its significance.

It could well be the case, though, that in the context of an emerging country such a formalised, structured and deliberate behaviour pattern is in fact an entirely new concept. Taking this example it could be a useful experience to explore the possibility that such a concept offers as a vehicle for learning and as an indication of the ready availability of resources that can be recycled in a new context.

---

12 For further implications see p. 136.

Diagrams and illustrative aids to learning under this heading are available in abundance but the one used here as Figure 2.14 is selected because it has the double-edged advantage of on the one hand being free from cultural overtones and on the other hand being readily useful as an aid to promote intelligent and guided discussion on those problems that can and do arise from cultural differences. This point is further explored in Chapter 3.[13]

Figure 2.14　　Communications analogue

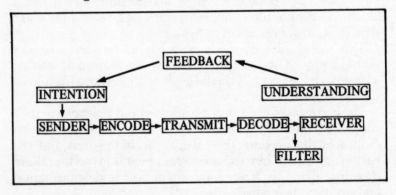

This aspect of the diagram is already useful in providing words that can be identified as representing total concepts. By being defined and understood they can make discussion possible:

SENDER　　　　'Has the responsibility for reception. There-fore must take into account all aspects of the receiver's background, attitudes, pre-conceptions and ability to understand.'

ENCODE　　　　'In selecting the method of communi-cation and the language to be used an effort must be made to make this ac-ceptable to the receiver.'

TRANSMIT　　　'The moment of transmission is the last chance to check that all possible steps have been taken to encourage understanding.'

---

13 For acknowledgement of this material please see the Reference note, p. 241.

DECODE   'Before the intention of the communication is absorbed by the receiver it will be
subject to a process of decoding according
to the level of understanding and to the
attitudes existing even before the effort to
communicate was begun.'

FILTER   'Other devices that can prevent understanding of an intention can be created by
a tone of voice, a superior attitude or by a
simple shrug of shoulders. Bias, preconceived ideas, latent inferiority complexes
are other examples of the whole set of
attitudes that if not taken into account when
formulating the intention, will become
barriers and filters to communication.'

RECEIVER   'Understanding the receiver is the first
step in trying to communicate with him.'

FEEDBACK   'In a verbal communication the moment
of intended reception of the communication presents the ideal time for checking
that the intention has been understood.
That moment can be the focal point for
final clarity and explanation.'

Here there is a wealth of material for achieving
maximum meaningful understanding:

- Such a simple backdrop can be used to underline the
importance of active listening.
- It pins down and acknowledges the responsibility for
communication.
- It highlights once again the need for prior knowledge
of people.
- Such an approach can readily be used as a visual aid to
discussion both within and between cultural groups.
- Because the content of the illustration is culture free it
can in fact be used to stimulate frank discussion about
the implementations of cultural differences.[14]

With the addition of examples an illustration that may at

---

14 These concepts are further expanded on pp. 55–72.

first appear to be totally theoretical can rather easily be made dynamic and useful.

- Frank reference to accent or other language difficulty can immediately avoid what could otherwise be a problem.
- Use of blanket words like 'they' or offensive words like 'boy' can be placed on the table as filters and discussed without emotion under that heading.
- Reasons for bias can be openly discussed.
- Latently emotional phrases like labour turnover and cost reduction can be replaced by others such as staff retention and selective spending.

Perhaps above all this example can be seen as one that clearly respects the intelligence of all parties to the learning process. It can be an important agent for creating a feeling of mutual trust and respect. Just as it can offer easy evidence of an open rather than a closed mind it can also be used to stimulate the openness of discussion that exposes problems before they have a chance to develop.

'Communication' is perhaps an easy example on which to build but there are many others that are just as easy, as appropriate and as reality-related. 'Behaviour' has already been illustrated as a concept and clearly many of the same points could apply if that chart were utilised as a backdrop.[15]

For the purpose of providing a further example a side step is taken into an area that could be considered to be one of the most difficult phases of learning – 'leadership'. Again, here there is a readily available resource which can be environment-related and stimulating and which can be used to develop, increase and extend understanding.

In this case the vehicle used is of British origin and must rank as being near the ultimate in terms of desophistication. In formal terms the illustration derives from a concept developed under the heading of 'The task approach to leadership'. It can best be seen within the framework of the

---

15 The concept presented here was developed by Dr John Adair in his book *Training for Leadership*, published by Macdonald & Co. Ltd., London. Both this work and his two books *Training for Communication* and *Training for Decisions* are recommended further reading. Please also see p. 241.

fulfilment of an objective through group and individual motivation.[16]

Figure 2.15 Task approach to leadership

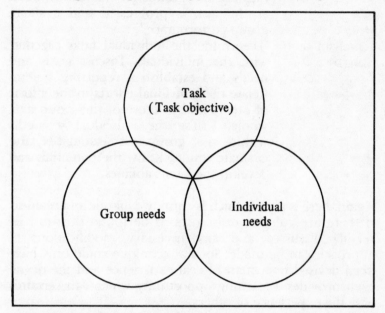

The basic illustration shown as Figure 2.15 contains its own clarity. The art of supervision is presented as the skill of keeping the three circles in balance. An important factor of this 'three-circle' approach is that it can be discussed at any level.

To develop the concept briefly:

TASK   'It is concerned with definition and direction and with the goals and over-all task settings. It can be seen in relation with other tasks and as a source of both broad-based and finite planning. It can be a backdrop for looking at needs and resources and in the context of the diagram can be seen as the main force for motivation.'

16 See also p. 20.

GROUP NEEDS   'Inform the group of the necessity of the task. Establish deadlines and set standards, leaving room for initiative and discussion. Enthuse the group. Provide information as the task is progressed and evaluate group performance.'

INDIVIDUAL   'Determine the individual tasks together
NEEDS   with the individuals. Discuss goals and needs and establish a reporting system. Relate the individual efforts to the efforts of others and to those of the group as a whole. Utilise the individual strengths within the group. Set standards and evaluate results. Know the potentials and develop the latent abilities.'

Again, here is a tool which is entirely dynamic and realistic. If there are cultural resistances to be found they can be readily discussed and any necessary modifications of approach can be made. Such a technique could only have been devised by a man of real experience and the device itself provides a learning opportunity which can certainly ease the experience of others.

The significant point about these aids to learning is that they provide opportunities for discussions which can be guided and directed so that they portray the living and dynamic aspects of relating with people. There is an implicit 'warmth' in the concepts themselves which is founded on the desire to understand. There is also an inbuilt element of trust which rests on the underlying theme of mutual respect. All of these are key words and like 'communications' they represent a set of values which, if carefully introduced into the language of any organisation, can become normal elements of the 'culture' of that organisation.

Again this is clear evidence that the emerging countries have the advantage as they can precalculate and strive towards the particular 'in-company' culture that best reflects their values. The two implications here are equally important:

● that the pre-knowledge of the environment includes a

thorough and penetrating pre-knowledge of the capacitiies and potentials of the people;
- that the resources are just as thoroughly examined from the points of view of appropriateness and application.

The key concept

Two important points made earlier were that the development of people is an accomplishment-oriented investment in the future, and that one of the essential skills in an emerging country is having the dual ability of depth of knowledge and the skill to make it meaningful.

The point to be added is that the advantage of the approaches presented, and of those that follow in greater detail in Chapter 3, is that they

- can be presented in a way that reduces the particular subject to its fundamental elements;
- are sufficiently desophisticated without the sacrifice of any of the key issues.
- can be used as aids to learning within almost all cultures.
- can be developed in content according to the needs.

It is the last of these points which provides the key to the really dynamic aspect and with that as a focal point the following comment is presented as a summary of the essential elements:

In initiating a learning experience any method used should first deal with the fundamentals. It must give deep consideration to the possible cultural aspects. It must be results-related in such a way that it contributes to a sense of achievement. While it should be concerned with stretching abilities it should also be focused on understanding. It must be capable of logical and progressive extension to the more sophisticated areas of the subject.

Such a statement can readily be used as a part of the job

profile of a manager at any level who has the responsibility to implement the learning process:

- He must have depth of knowledge in at least one specific field.
- He must be able to reduce it to the appropriate level of understanding.
- He must be able to stretch the abilities of others in a way that motivates them.
- He must be able to extend the level of learning.

As an example of what is intended it will be clear that the 'three circles', in the last example of the previous section, can be supplemented, according to the requirements, and to the appropriate level of understanding, by

- organisation profile studies
- group dynamics
- management-style analysis
- performance-standard task setting
- management by objectives
- motivation studies
- task team approaches etc.

The foundation for each of these exists in the initial learning. The earlier 'behaviour' illustration as well as the 'communications analogue' can be extended in the same manner so that the total process, including both the initial illustrative aid and all of its extensions, can be regarded as a single on-going learning process.

The concepts are founded on and designed to encourage change. They can incorporate both hard facts and visions. New learning is based on the reinforcement of previous learning.

Conclusion

- Rather than theory-based teaching, what is required is learning that is meaningful and ideas that can be communicated as being achievable.
- One of the essential skills in promoting learning is the ability to strip new knowledge of its non-essential sophistications so that it can be understood within a given set of personal relationships.
- It is critical that the intelligence of all those involved in

the learning process is respected and that there is an emerging belief in the fact that individual capacities can be expanded.

- New knowledge can most effectively be communicated within the context of the living facts of the daily environment.
- National pride is a vital force for growth when it is sustained by reasons to remain proud that are viable and built on growth, understanding, self-respect and respect for others.
- Giving people a future vision of their environment and of themselves in relation to the dynamism of that environment can be the most effective medium for making changes possible.
- Through this integration of vision both the learning and the change process can be made meaningful.
- The essential concern is to present knowledge within the broad conceptual framework of people development in such a way that it is meaningful, in context and motivating.
- The act of charting the processes of management can provide both understanding of an existing situation and can reveal possibilities for change within the application of the processes.
- Presenting management in terms of its components can be accomplished without sacrifice of the realism that operational management is a living process that changes as situations change.
- By analysing management in terms of its relationship with accomplishment the concept of organisation can be seen as being derived from purpose and goals rather than as an imposed set of restrictive constraints.
- Similarly the concept of organisation can be used to show how a vision can be given shape and dimension, and how tasks can be made supportive to the achievement of the vision.
- Practical training and development needs are best stated in terms of the current and projected organisation from a structural, a quantitative and a qualitative point of view.

- Analysis of the priorities and of specific need areas is fundamental to the design of a training and development philosophy that will avoid *ad hoc* approaches and make the total effort more effective.
- Just as points of common interest will emerge between companies within one environment, there will be common denominators between similar countries.
- In terms of resources it will be found that the experiences in one country can provide useful inputs for overcoming the problems in another country.
- This aspect of resource-sharing or cross-cultural applicability of resources highlights the requirement for a precise definition of needs to be accompanied by skilful application of the resource inputs.
- The greatest danger in the learning process is the assumption of a level of knowledge that does not in fact exist.
- The greatest aids to the learning process are those which are environment-related, stimulating, and directed towards developing understanding.
- In illustrating and discussing the concepts and components of management the value system within the in-company culture can to a large extent be predetermined.
- Ideally new knowledge should be presented in a way that reduces the subject to its fundamental elements, without sacrifice of any of the key issues, and provides a foundation for logical and progressive extention to the more sophisticated areas of the subject.
- Training and development must be seen as a dynamic system or process which is comprehensive and continuous, which exists in the context of the purpose of an organisation or institution, and which exists in the context of a particular country.

3 Practical aids

Implementation against a planned background

Once there is a clear understanding of the needs and priorities, the logical progressive steps can be planned. Such a step series will depend on many circumstances, but the essential point is that the whole training and people development activity is likely to prove most effective when it is placed in the context of a plan.[1]

The following three-phase approach is a practical example of a background plan that has been used with some success in a number of distinctly different countries.

The three phases are:
a language phase
a function or skills phase
a managing phase.

Phase 1 – Language

This concentrates initial attention on obtaining a common understanding of the words, expressions and abbreviations commonly used in the organisation.

With this as a first step people at whatever level who join the organisation can at least speak its language and gain some early feeling of identity. Also in this phase the various expressions relating to normal daily management practice can be introduced and made meaningful. A critical aspect of this language phase is its contribution to the formation of a deliberately structured in-organisation culture. Clearly,

---

1 Extensions of this planned approach are further exampled in Chapter 4.

failure to recognise the importance of this first phase can lead to many problems in later development efforts and, at the same time, can result in both confusion and embarrassment, which is no fault of the people being trained and developed.

On the other hand the advantages can readily be exampled. The level of 'communications' in an organisation where all parties have the same basic understanding of the word must benefit. The climate in an organisation where 'empathy' is a word appearing in all initial training programmes must contain more natural efforts directed towards understanding.[2] Planning will not be a mysterious process if its basic purpose and its place as a normal management component has been discussed. There is likely to be a greater degree of trust emerging from a situation where a deliberate effort is made to introduce the people, the policies, the procedures and the purpose of the organisation as a normal and integral step in the initial period.

This whole phase can be further reinforced by explanation of the traditions of the company. When these are intermixed with stories of a country's or an organisation's personalities, stories of battles or contracts won and lost, and stories of the growing together of a set of interests and values, a feeling of age, permanence and belonging will be added. Such backgrounds will reinforce the integration of interests and of vision which can be shown to exist between the country, the economy, the organisation or institution and the individuals. Certainly it is reasonable to expect that people trained and educated in the philosophy of any enterprise are more likely to have a later intuitive reaction to problems that will reflect their understanding of its attitudes and ethics.

Phase 2 – Function or skills

This focuses attention on the technical aspect of tasks in terms of processes, procedures and methods, in so far as

---

2 Further substance is added by the examples on pp. 149 and 167.

these are appropriate to the environment and can be developed and demonstrated.

This is perhaps the most important phase in terms of impact on the people and in terms of initial motivation and self-confidence. Seen from the broadest base this phase can include the sending of selected staff to more developed, or more experienced, neighbouring countries for the development of basic skills and supervisory training. It can include the development, together, of local selling and service techniques and methods; it can incorporate the building up, together, of the various manuals concerning procedures. In these ways people are given the means not only to carry out their assigned tasks but also the means to develop.

In this phase it is often necessary to dwell on the most fundamental elements as these are the critical factors when facing fundamental problems. Because the most practical and immediate training normally takes place on the job, extra care must be devoted to the on-the-job examples. Here the manager will be the most important single influence.[3]

One of the key points in this phase is that the managers, whether expatriate, foreign-trained or local, be prepared to expose their knowledge and be seen to be interested in building up the knowledge of their people. This in itself is a real test as this process of passing on knowledge of techniques and procedures demands a rare mix of abilities – to know when to be insistent, when to be patient – and to convey an attitude that others can learn from and copy. People in emerging countries are not necessarily less intelligent or less innovative, neither are they less sensitive or less adaptable. They may well be less familiar with things taken for granted in developed countries, but, in total, the advantage is that they are generally receptive to new learning and new ideas. Such people have to be made to feel that their opinion is important and that their initiatives are welcome. Certainly there are times where a manager must be insistent and it is on those occasions that he can make his greatest contribution.

---

3 This aspect of example setting is placed in context on p. 144.

Skill in such cases can add a sense of discipline, and explanation of why something has to be done in a particular way can be a critical factor and can help to induce a feeling for self-discipline. The art of criticism also presents a new challenge as even the impression of looking over a man's shoulder can promote a sense of sheer terror for the man whose self-respect may well depend on how well he copes with a newly acquired skill.

Phase 3 – Managing

This is concerned with conveying the various conceptual aspects of management.

Here the vital point to be recognised is that nothing is gained by avoiding issues. In those cases involving the use of foreign staff in key positions this is an area where frank and open discussion can provide possibilities for joint and mutual understanding. To repeat the example, the whole concept of communication can be complex enough in a small office, but when such a process is subject to interpretation through language, culture, and patterns of social discipline, problems can only be solved by discussion of the differences. At this point the benefits of the first phase become apparent as great care has to be taken with the common understanding of key words.

A local language that has been developed in an environment dominated by the size of a catch of fish or the quality of a rice paddy irrigation system will not necessarily have developed a code or language suitable for the finer points of modern business. Relatively non-emotive expressions in one country can be emotion-loaded in another. 'Democracy' and 'democratic principles' may be harmless enough as concepts but there are many countries where they are cut-off points to any conversation. The requirement here is not to ignore the concepts but to find words that are appropriate.

It is an unfortunate fact that many daily relationships, when formalised, structured and presented as deliberate processes or patterns, tend to reappear as entirely new concepts. As was illustrated in Figure 2.1 on p. 12, the components, contents and the concepts can best be presented within the context of the business cycle. In this way they can be given meaning within the constraints of the environment.

While the example provided in Table 3.1 is reality-based in the sense that it has been used many times as a backdrop, it is entirely flexible. While the first phase will be the easiest where it is introduced at the outset of a project it could be the most difficult when introduced into an on-going situation.

Ideally, the input of information should flow at a controlled and increasing rate so that learning is progressive. On the other hand there is also a 'need to know' factor which dictates that some people will require to progress quickly to the third phase, while others must be progressed as rapidly as possible in their skills training.

Also ideally, the approach exampled under the heading of 'highly structured and open-ended' should be used on a selective basis in both the second and third phases. Time, however, may demand that in the initial stages a simple 'instruction' approach be used to ensure that all are starting on the same base.

The essential point however is that wherever possible a planned approach be used. Within the constraints imposed by the realities of time and the need to know, development has to proceed through the stage of learning to understand the process of change to the stage of learning how to influence change in terms of goal-setting and resource utilisation. This element of dynamism has therefore to be added to the planned approach and the further underlining point is that people development is concerned not only with the need to provide an appreciation of methods, techniques, and systems but also with the skills of applying and using them – sometimes in a resistant society. The more thorough the learning process the more likely it is that through the development of a core of motivated people such resistance can be overcome. To take it one step further local people are always the experts in local situations and their development is the only way to overcome local resistance.

Table 3.1 Example of the planned three-phase approach

(i) 'Language phase' to include

- Introduction to the enterprise in terms of its
    - People
    - Principles
    - Practices
    - Procedures
    - Policies
    - Philosophy
- Brief introduction to the essential concepts
- Introduction to the internal language and abbreviations
- Introduction to the management processes and the inter-dependent roles of the various functions.

(ii) 'Functional or Skills phase' to include

- Through a mix of open-ended and closed seminars built around the current and projected operating processes
    - Technical training
    - Basics of selling
    - Planning and forecasting
    - Understanding economics
    - Cost awareness
    - Basics of supervision
    - Providing a service
- Skills training on and off the job
- Developing skills in others

(iii) 'Managing phase' to include

- Discussions regarding the components and concepts of managing, namely
    - Motivation
    - Leadership
    - Communication
    - Counselling
    - People development

Phase (i) as an introductory programme to be repeated as and when necessary.

Phase (ii) as follow up to be programmed annually.

Phase (iii) according to requirements.

Highly structured and open-ended

Just as it is fundamental that wherever possible the implementation of training and development programmes should take place according to a plan, a further basic essential to successful implementation is that it be environment-related.

In terms of the definition provided in Chapter 2 the most critical points in initiating any learning experience were shown to be that:

- The method used should first deal with the fundamentals.
- It must give deep consideration to the possible cultural aspects.
- It must be results-related in such a way that it contributes a sense of achievement.
- It should be concerned with stretching abilities.
- It should be focused on understanding.
- It must be capable of logical and progressive extention to the more sophisticated areas of any specific subject.

Other critical key points emerging in Chapter 2 that are relevant under this very important heading were:

- What is required is learning that is meaningful and ideas that can be communicated as being achievable.
- In the first phase of transferring new learning it must be stripped of any non-essential sophistications that could in any way limit its understanding.
- It is critical that the learning method should respect the intelligence of all those involved in the learning process.
- The method must also ensure that there is an emerging belief in the fact that individual capacities can be expanded.
- New knowledge can most effectively be communicated within the context of the living facts of the daily environment by a learning process that is environment-related, stimulating and directed towards obtaining understanding.

'Highly structured and open-ended' is an abbreviation of a total method which will be described in detail in the following pages. As a summary of the intention of the method it could initially be described as being the development of a firmly designed frame of reference within which discussion can be guided at any desired level. The method can be used to satisfy all of the requirements specified in the preceding pages.

The example used here refers to a programme produced under the heading of 'the role and work of supervisor' and in this case the structured aspect of the programme is provided by a set of basic learning inputs as follows:

Introductory Segment–	Relating the role of the supervisor to the process of management
Segment 1	– The concept of leadership
Segment 2	– Planning and structured organisation
Segment 3	– Motivating
Segment 4	– Communicating
Segment 5	– Controlling and disciplining
Segment 6	– Employee relations and morale
Segment 7	– Decision-making and problem-solving
Segment 8	– Objective and standard setting
Segment 9	– Training
Segment 10	– Safety
Segment 11	– Interviewing and counselling
Segment 12	– Control systems
Concluding Segment	– Review and evaluation

Each segment accounts for four hours of input learning and discussion.

For each segment the input includes selected pre-readings which can be translated where necessary, a set of topic notes which provide the in-course materials and set the standards of knowledge to be transmitted within the segment heading, a set of guides for discussion which are intended to obtain job-related and environment-related responses, and in some cases a set of follow-up readings.

In using this resource material there is room for further selection so that programmes can be directed towards any given level of understanding.

Important points in regard to the programme are as follows:

- The opening segment provides a general business setting with specific references to the realities of the particular situation. It is intended that this segment will localise the management process and acknowledge the environmental constraints from the outset.
- Each segment contains many participative opportunities so that the input content is channelled into discussion of localised problems.
- While the presentation is guided by the topic notes, the intention is to provide a free-style approach. In this way the focusing of the inputs is left to the person conducting the programme.
- Supplemental support material can be provided for all segments so that the level of the inputs can be better directed towards the level of understanding of the participants. Further, the level of the input can readily be controlled by the person conducting the programme, enabling him to concentrate on particular aspects and to achieve results in recognised problem areas.
- Additions can readily be made to the supplementary support content to ensure that the total inputs are regularly updated.
- Each learning step is reinforced both by the discussions and by controlled repetition in the later segments. Supplemental reinforcement can be provided by questioning the participants at the conclusion of each segment regarding the practical application of a new knowledge input.
- While the structuring can allow for variety in the style of presentation of each segment, the basic pattern is intended to remain reasonably uniform – that is, work-centred pre-reading, review of pre-reading, introduction of selected new material and discussion.
- The programme can be designed in such a way that it can be used by any experienced manager. The pre-reading, handouts, notes for reinforcement and points for flip chart or blackboard use can be readily structured.

In terms of learning theory certain guiding criteria have been considered in building up this approach. Notably the main points have been:
- Adults are said to learn more effectively when they can participate in setting the pace of their learning.
- Individuals will make a greater learning effort if they can recognise the latent benefits.
- Learning is optimised when it is active rather than passive.
- Learning methods need to be varied.
- Intermittent opportunities should be provided to practise what has been learned.
- Adults prefer practical application rather than tests of learning achievement.
- Idea-input methods should be accompanied by channels for feedback.
- Learning reinforcement is an essential element of continuity.
- Discussion of recognisable situations provides the optimum climate for group learning.
- Changed individual behaviour reinforcement is best achieved through group feedback and reinforcement.

The examples that follow as Tables 3.2 – 3.5 have been extracted from 'Communicating', Segment 4 of the programme. This material has been selected for this purpose because of its almost universal relevance to supervisory training and because it can be immediately useful as resource input for this purpose. The example material also serves to illustrate the point that the preparation of such input, particularly for a supervisory group, is not difficult and can in many cases be accomplished by utilising readily available input materials. It will also be noted that the material is complementary to that already made available in Chapter 2.[4]

The pre-reading examples given as Tables 3.2, 3.3, 3.4 and 3.5 have been selected from the supervisory inputs. Those that are available as pre-reading for a management-oriented group are set at a higher level and are both more academic and more deliberately provocative.

---

4 For reference see p. 36.

Table 3.2 Communicating: Pre-reading 1

From Segment 1 we know that management/supervision is concerned with reaching a predetermined objective through the efforts of other people.

From Segment 2 we are aware of the processes of reporting, delegating, planning and the relationship with own accomplishment.

From Segment 3 we know that a motive is something that creates the urge to react to a particular need.

We know the significance of the development gap and how it can influence accomplishment. We know that it is our responsibility to close the gap.

We know that a satisfied need is no longer a useful motivator.

We are aware of the various environmental forces that affect behaviour.

From our daily experience we know that achievement of results through people is only possible if we have an understanding of both behaviour and motivation.

From our daily experience we also know that to get things done we have to relate with and communicate with other people.

As experienced supervisors we are daily engaged in the art of communicating.

Table 3.3 Communicating: Pre-reading 2 (an individual exercise)

Assuming that we know what we want done and when we want it done, why is it that our subordinates fail to live up to our expectations?

....

....

....

....

....

....

The greatest frustration in the daily life of any supervisor in this country is?

....

....

....

....

....

....

The information that I need to know to successfully perform my function can be listed as follows:

....

....

....

....

....

....

Table 3.4 Communicating: Pre-reading 3 (an individual exercise)

Please comment on the validity of the following statements:

Communication can be defined as the act of sending information from one person to another person.

....
....

A person who is fully familiar with his subject will be able to communicate it.

....
....

People in this country are not basically interested in anything outside their own jobs.

....
....

If people want to know more they will ask.

....
....

A supervisor will lose face if he asks his staff for their suggestions.

....
....

Giving personal advice to his staff is an integral part of a supervisor's task.

....
....

In communicating a job to be performed it is important to communicate the smallest details.

....
....

It will help the subordinate's concentration if the supervisor does not allow interruptions when giving instruction.

....
....

The ability to communicate well cannot be taught.

....
....

Table 3.5 Communicating: Pre-reading 4 (an individual exercise)

The most difficult aspect of work-related communication in this country is:

....

....

....

....

....

....

....

....

....

....

....

....

Because? ....

....

....

....

....

....

....

....

....

....

....

....

....

....

At the commencement of the four-hour input and discussion session one of the many one-way/two-way communications exercises is conducted. These can vary widely in presentation but the usual format is to create a situation where one man is instructing a group from a prepared script, normally to sketch a relatively complex design. This is done first as a monologue and later with the opportunity to ask questions. The result is that the two-way communication provides for more effective message reception. The situation can readily be localised by amending the content of the instruction to sketch something which will be culturally recognisable, such as a local craft design.

This is followed by a sub-division into small groups to discuss the results of the pre-readings and to derive brief reports for a group plenary discussion.

Already at this stage of such an exercise the learning process has a local flavour and can be directed in terms of both depth and breadth of coverage.

Another useful aid to force localisation of discussion is to request the small discussion groups jointly to note ten local proverbs or sayings that provide a fair expression of the local way of life. The chosen proverbs or sayings should ideally be expressive of the inbuilt attitudes to group or individual effort. Again, using this device the discussions that follow can be channelled in many directions, not the least important of which could be concerned with the difficulties of translation when communicating attitudes and feelings.

From Tables 3.6 – 3.14 it will be clear that the open-ended element can be readily induced from a rather structured approach. For more senior groups the input data can be retained and supplemented and the discussion papers can be even less structured so as to obtain a more free-style set of responses.

One of the basic assumptions in this presentation is that it takes place in phase three of a planned approach. This is an important aspect, as the assumption implies that the internal language is understood and that the skill to perform assigned tasks is present in all participants.

Table 3.6 Communicating: Input 1: Definition

Stated very briefly 'communications' in the management sense refers to the flow of ideas, instructions and information and of the capacity of an individual or group to pass on ideas and feelings to another individual or group.

This concept includes:

    (a)   Transmission of orders and instructions from employer to employee.

    (b)   Transmission of reports and ideas, suggestions and complaints, and other dissatisfactions or grievances, whether real or fancied, from employees to employer.

    (c)   Cross-communication between group members.

    (d)   Communication by extra-company groups, e.g. the union or the family.

This concept of employee communication is vital because it offers a medium aiding effective co-ordination. If we assume that the ability to perform exists through the proper provision of tools and skills, co-ordination results because employees know <u>what to do</u> and have the <u>will to do</u>.

They learn what to do from orders and instructions and their knowledge of on-the-job objectives.

Very briefly there are three basic stages of arousing interest by information:

    (a)   Instructions in the significance of the job the employee will do or is doing and how it affects the work of others and the work of the company as a whole.

    (b)   The purpose of the job clearly understood.

    (c)   On-the-job training, i.e. how to do the job.

They, therefore, have the will to do from their understanding of the relationship between the employee's own interest, their work environment and their own self-interest.

Table 3.7   Communicating: Input 2: Dual purpose

From what has already been said it is clear that employee
communications has as its purpose:

(a)   To convey orders and instructions making
         possible the performance of work in accordance
         with set standards.
(b)   To convey information and understanding to
         achieve willing co-operation. The first of these
         can be called formal communication; that is,
         through the line structure of the organisation.

Requirements of this form of communication are that they
must be:

(a)   Authentic
(b)   Authoritative
(c)   Intelligible
(d)   Planned-for and followed up

Key points regarding the communication of instructions are:

(a)   Plan and prepare for the order with an objective
         in mind.
(b)   Be sure that the order receiver has the ability and
         facilities to carry out the order.
(c)   Recognise that the way in which an order is given
         will affect the result.
(d)   Make the order important in the mind of the
         receiver.
(e)   Make the order complete.
(f)   Back up the order with facts that explain why it
         is necessary.
(g)   Let the receiver know by what criteria he will be
         judged, i.e. specify a standard.
(h)   Verify reception of the order, i.e. ensure that
         it is understood.

Table 3.7   continued

To a large degree co-ordination and co-operation depend upon
adequate communication between all levels and in all areas.
Communication is therefore a prerequisite to effective operation
because any organisation has little chance of co-ordinating its
activities without it. Built into this 'will to do' is a sense of
purpose and a sense of participation in something that is
worthwhile and worth doing.

Some of the ways in which communication seeks to build a
feeling of integration and the will to do are:

(a) By providing an understanding of the social
environment of the company.

(b) By providing an understanding of the company's
policies and goals.

(c) By providing an understanding of the employees'
function in the company. Through work the
employees' personal objectives need to be
related to the company's objectives.

(d) By promoting understanding between employee
groups.

(e) By providing expanded knowledge.

(f) By showing personal understanding in both a
social and a technical sense.

This can perhaps best be summed up by saying that a part of
every manager's job is to motivate and communicate. His job
is to make a team out of his people and this is primarily a
social skill.

Table 3.8 Communicating: Discussion guide 1 (for small group and plenary discussion)

Effective communication is important for:
Controlling, because ....
....
....
....

Co-ordinating, because ....
....
....
....

Delegating, because ....
....
....
....

Motivating, because ....
....
....
....

Reporting, because ....
....
....
....

Ineffective upward communication will result in ....
....
....

Ineffective communication with subordinates will result in ...
....
....

The most essential point in communicating is ....
....
....
....
....
....

Table 3.9 Communicating: Input 3: Value of keeping people informed

Communications when applied as an integral part of normal management can:

(a) Contribute to efficiency.

(b) Make for an improved working environment.

(c) Contribute to improved morale.

(d) Contribute to the personal development of employees.

(e) Be a very real medium for both assessing and perhaps changing employee attitudes.

(f) Provide employees with a means of expression.

(g) Prompt employee loyalty and co-operation.

(h) Motivate employees.

(i) Inform management of employee needs and objectives and their reactions to the company's objectives, policies, etc.

(j) Interpret and explain company policy.

(k) Foster teamwork, co-operation, co-ordination.

(l) Counteract propaganda and rumour.

Table 3.10 Communicating: Discussion guide 2 (for small group and plenary discussion)

In this society the major factors that have to be considered as potential filters to the reception of communication are:

....

....

....

....

....

....

....

....

....

....

The most effective means of overcoming these filtering reactions are likely to be:

....

....

....

....

....

....

....

....

....

....

....

....

Table 3.11 Communicating: Input 5: Barriers to effective communications

Barriers to effective communications are usually due to the temperament of the man, such as shyness, pride because he wishes to keep things to himself and profit from matters which could interest others, and to other factors, such as physical overwork, acceptance of a continually accelerating tempo of work and lack of awareness of the importance of information in the assessment of priorities.

Some of the other barriers are mainly due to:

(a) Time

(b) Space.

(c) Division between departments or branches of a business.

(d) Conflicts due to social and cultural differences.

(e) Human sentiment, emotion and simple resistance to change.

(f) Differences in background, experience and motivation.

(g) Lack of personal understanding between people.

(h) Lack of example.

(i) Lack of persistence.

(j) Aloofness.

(k) Fear of reprisal.

(l) Lack of knowledge of authority.

(m) Lack of appreciation of other people's needs for information.

(n) The danger of assumption.

Table 3.11 continued

Some other attitudes here are:

(a) The legalistic attitude which consists of hiding behind rules or regulations.

(b) The 'sensible thing to do' attitude which is inadequate, often causing difficulty when it amounts to no more than intuition or impulse.

(c) Procrastination—an attitude very frequently encountered and one which often takes the place of a definite policy. This is the main cause of employees believing that all improvements must be forcibly extracted from an employer.

(d) Force—an attitude which results in continuous conflict. This often exists between and within branches, departments, section, etc. The real problem of course is not to discover who is the stronger but who is right.

(e) Paternalism which simply means satisfying needs by pure benevolence.

(f) Sharp practice—in other words ceaseless argument in an attempt to trick the other side. This of course hinders the growth of confidence and accentuates the selfish demands of the groups concerned. This attitude makes it practically impossible to find a common objective.

Table 3.12   Communicating: Discussion guide 3 (for small group and plenary discussion)

My ability as a communicator would be improved if I knew more about:

....

....

....

....

....

....

With my particular group I must:

....

....

....

....

....

....

The level of understanding of those responsible to me will improve if I:

....

....

....

....

....

....

....

Table 3.13 Communicating: Input 6: Making communications effective

Effective employer/employee communications is not merely telling or placing information at the disposal of other groups. Effective communication comes only from long and trustworthy personal interchange of information and sharing experiences so that people are brought to new problems in similar ways. This integration of interests must result between employer and employee so that both may work toward mutually designated objectives.

The principle of integrated interests is fundamental to effective employee communications because its lack will cause various segments of the organisation to work at cross-purposes.

The vital point is that employees need to know any information which will help them do a better job in the long run.

1 Encourage group spirit

Important factors here can be:

(a) Realisation of interdependence.
(b) Ready exchange of information regarding current events.
(c) Establishing a climate of mutual respect.
(d) Official and informal social integration.
(e) The creation of a feeling that staff belong.
(f) Increased opportunities for participation.

2 Ensure that all communication is understandable

Important points here are:

(a) That communication should be in terms of the receiver's background.
(b) To listen with understanding.
(c) To use understandable words and ideas.
(d) To develop an understandable style in speaking and writing.
(e) To arrange material for easy reading or listening.
(f) To communicate within a context.
(g) To communicate within the receiver's self-interest and at the same time acknowledge your own self-interest.
(h) That talking down produces negative responses.

Table 3.13   continued

(i)   That communication should have both a personal
      quality and alive interest, i.e. it must be personally
      relevant.
(j)   That each person's ability to communicate varies with
      his own understanding of the topic.
(k)   That the most effective communication material is that
      which the employees can recognise as affecting them
      personally.
(l)   That a good communication programme respects both
      the intelligence and the self-respect of employees.
(m)   That clearly stated, communication programmes can
      minimise the possibility of misunderstandings which
      are the main source of industrial dispute.

3   Recognise the means of obtaining information from staff

(a)   By providing encouragement.
(b)   By example to create the right attitude.
(c)   By keeping employees informed.
(d)   By always acknowledging ideas and suggestions.
(e)   By allowing for participation.
(f)   By realising that there is in fact a need for a two-way
      flow of information.
(g)   By creating a feeling of mutual confidence.

4   Recognise that limits do exist

These limits generally apply to:

(a)   Special material of a confidential nature.
(b)   The varying needs of different levels of staff.
(c)   The varying degrees of understanding within those
      levels.

Care should be taken with the distribution of information
so that it cannot be misinterpreted by its recipient and
cause subsequent rumour and confusion. Do not over-
communicate.

5   Be realistic about morale

Morale should be recognised as the drive to work well, rather
than as contentment.

Table 3.13   continued

It is obvious that every manager must communicate to fulfil
his purpose of getting things done through people and the
advantage of good communications is that things have a better
chance of getting done well and with good will.

While communications is by definition multidirectional it is
not necessarily spontaneous nor can it be improved by providing
just bigger, better and more information. One essential is a
feeling of trust and respect which can both stimulate and be
stimulated by good communications. The second essential is
that without a living example of communication downwards,
communication upwards will be impossible.

Further key aspects are:

(a)   Be sincere.

(b)   Be simple and unaffected in your language.

(c)   Do not over-glorify the company.

(d)   Make the task of keeping people informed a top-
level supervisory responsibility.

(e)   Do not ignore unsavoury situations which your
employees know to exist.

Table 3.14 Communicating: Discussion guide 4 (for small group and plenary discussion)

(To be completed individually and retained for later discussion with your manager.)

This segment was important to me because ....

....

....

....

....

....

I would still like to learn more about ....

....

....

....

....

As a means of improving this aspect within my own department I intend to ....

....

....

....

....

....

....

....

As a means of making this segment more relevant to local circumstances I would like to suggest ....

....

....

....

....

....

....

....

Other key points regarding the approach are:
- the relative ease of introducing reinforcement of learning content
- the provision of inputs that can be summarised for prior flip chart presentation and can be used as handout materials
- the combination of the personalised, localised and commitment aspects
- the value placed on the opinions of participants
- the repeated use of a feedback approach
- the use of the small group discussions to assist in the coaching process of individuals
- the use of the discussion papers to ensure that all participants will form opinions
- the implied use of the plenary sessions to encourage summarising and reporting skills
- the deliberate reference back to the normal chain of command which is implicit in the final question in the last small group and plenary discussion paper.

Three further examples are given. The first, Figure 3.1 (Input 4 from the segment concerning interviewing), is of interest because of its frank statement concerning 'barriers'. While the validity of the points made is apparent within the emerging country context, they are probably equally valid within any other context where the same differences exist but in a less pronounced form.

The second, Table 3.15 (Input 3 in the interviewing and counselling segment), provides an example of a deceptively simple discussion backdrop. It is given specific mention here because it is a good illustration of an instrument that can be used to probe rather deeply into the conditioning aspects of environment. In this case the device of the six-factor approach is far from original and also illustrates the fact of the plentiful supply of input resources that are available.

The discussion on the title 'Manager' (Table 3.16) is from the introductory segment and creates an immediate confrontation situation with those managers in many of the emerging countries who are content with the title alone and see it as reason enough for the private office and the not less private secretary. The last sentence of the first half of the input provides an easy entry for a good level of discussion of

Figure 3.1   Interviewing and counselling: The aim of
interview conversation[5]

While the principle objective concerns the exchange of information
this is only possible if there is some mutuality of understanding.

Patience
Care
Self Knowledge
System
Understanding
Tact
Willingness to listen

THE BARRIER

DIFFERENCES IN
EXPERIENCE
CULTURE
AGE
EDUCATION
MOTIVATION
ENVIRONMENT
PERSPECTIVE

Mutuality
of
Understanding

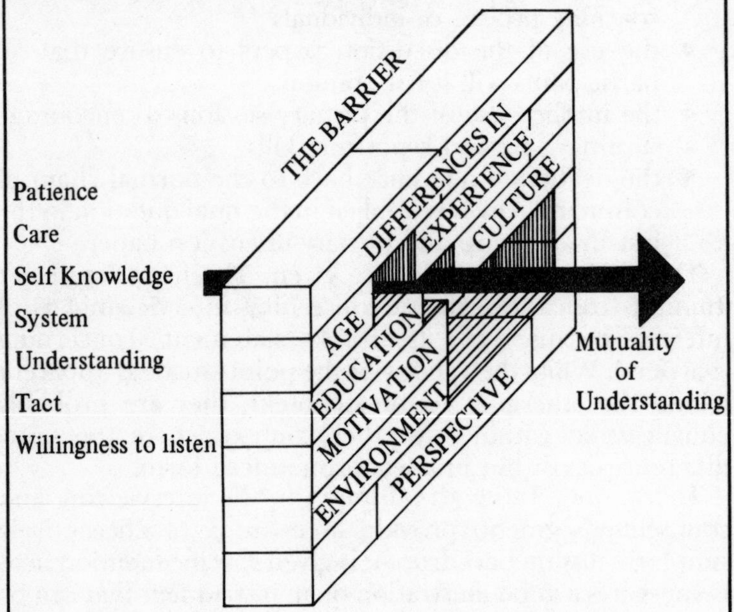

The barriers can vary in both size and content but once they are
recognised it is important to realise that they can be overcome.

5 See also pp. 90–102.

Table 3.15   Interviewing and counselling: Input 3: Behaviour[6]

Essentially, it is necessary to understand that there are six basic facts which apply equally to all people. Stated very briefly, they are:

1   Every individual has been conditioned by his past experience (the manager therefore requires to know something of the particular person's past).

2   Every individual is in a present situation (the manager therefore must know the everyday situation and the normal reaction to it).

3   From the conditioning results of past experience, individuals develop certain demands which they make in their present situation.

4   Their present situations are making certain demands on individuals.

5   It is important to recognise therefore, that every individual is adjusting himself to these two pressures:

     (a)   His expectation from the job.

     (b)   The pressure that the job exerts on him.

6   It is fundamental that the conflict of demands can be resolved (the real difficulty here for the manager is getting the true nature of the demands clearly revealed. This in itself, provides one aspect of the need for the appraisal development interview).

---

6 For acknowledgement of this material please see the Reference note, p. 241.

Table 3.16 Introductory segment: Input 2: The title 'Manager'

The title 'Manager' does not carry with it the skill to manage or the ability to lead. Management and leadership are complex skills that require learning and the real evidence that they exist in any person comes not only from the short-term results but from the attitude and respect of those who are managed.

A manager exists in a business environment and his task is to achieve results through the efforts of others in that environment. To be successful in achieving his objectives he must recognise that the motives of his people may be different from his own and that his own progress depends on his understanding of these differences. His ability to motivate and involve his people with his and the company's objectives are the real indicators of his ability.

Effective leadership and motivation should not be confused with keeping people 'happy' and 'contented'. The goal is to keep people active and striving while at the same time holding their interest and encouraging a feeling of involvement. Essentially it is a matter of giving people the 'will to work well' and providing a feeling of accomplishment.

Mature employees at any level realise that a business exists to meet objectives of profit, productivity and continuity and such people are prepared to work well towards such goals provided their own goals are acknowledged and provided for.

In fact the needs of his people are not so different from the needs of the manager. All require a sense of belonging, integration and identity, together with an opportunity to exercise social and personal skills within a particular level of competence.

the Katz essay on the 'Skills of an Effective Administrator' which in itself can be provided as excellent pre-reading for a manager group.

The second half of the input provides for early identity of a work-orientated definition of morale and at the same time introduces the concept of profit in relation to continuity. The highly structured and open-ended approach exampled here by supervisory-level extracts has been used in a number of very different situations.

In one case the 'role and work of the supervisor' with its many hundreds of possible inputs and discussion leads was used by the manager of a 3000-man plant as a basic resource for a series of total organisation programmes. Making full use of the open-ended approach, resource selections were made initially for the most senior local staff and two further sets of selections were later made for two levels of supervisors. An interesting aspect of this exercise was that in some cases the discussion leads were rewritten to focus on the exposure of the known existing problems as it was felt that many of these would prove to be common to a number of the participants and could best be resolved by group or plenary discussion. As this was also an on-going situation in a climate of spectacular growth the opportunity was also taken to reinforce the in-company language so that the earlier neglect of the phase 1 sector was rectified.

In other cases resource selections have been done by personnel managers as a means of structuring 'Basics of Management' programmes. Again, in these cases both the input and the discussion leads have served as a vehicle to focus attention on the optimum viability of existing methods and procedures in many sectors of the enterprise.

In all cases where the method has been applied its particular merit has been its usefulness as a practical and non-emotive means for probing and exploring the people-oriented environmental demands on management. This is no way restricted to the foreign or expatriate manager but is equally applicable to the local manager in a country where there are cultural and behavioural differences within the society. Such differences do occur in many countries and cannot be ignored when organisations or institutions become nation-wide. Knowledge of the differences is also important for the local man who has studied or acquired his management training abroad, as in this case it can be a matter of adapting learning to 'new' circumstances.

Further aids to localising

Referring back to the problem of resources it can often be necessary to apply on-the-spot inventiveness, imagination and creativity.

Too little courage and too much patience in this regard can too easily become an excuse to either do nothing or to use merely the standard approaches, which are not always appropriate. Clearly, people with an expectation of a learning experience will be sensitive and any self-doubts on the part of those responsible will very easily be transferred to those being trained.

As an alternative there will be cases when it is reasonable to state that, for example, 'we are not quite sure of the appropriateness of this method, aid, film, case, etc., but let's try it and see if, together, we can find a way to make it useful'. This involvement approach will certainly produce its failures but it is unlikely to produce disasters. Where there are no other alternatives it will be preferable to taking a non-acknowledged uncertain step and is certainly preferable to taking no action at all.

When viewed in this way the task is to create together a local understanding of whatever may be locally useful from whatever source material is available. In this regard the true experts are the local people. Case studies present a very practical example. Just as there can be resistance to foreign accents and mannerisms, there can certainly be resistance to case studies that are based on conditions of life entirely foreign to a local situation. Where there is no other solution the suggestion here is to proceed with the case by asking the participants to rewrite it in a way that takes account of the local circumstances. While some may see this approach as an abuse of the case-study method, it is on the other hand, an alternative method of learning which focuses on the localisation of a situation and at the same time provides a locally based resource which can be used by others. As a further adaptation of this example it can also be a useful deliberate exercise for study groups or task groups to use the same approach and produce a selection of localised case studies.

Many other approaches can be used and a number of these are listed below:

- Providing reporting assignments to small groups of course participants. This has the advantage of providing feedback and it also provides the particular participants with a greater sense of involvement.
- Setting group or individual assignments to create brief case-study inputs on the basis of their daily tasks. In this way there will be a constant input of local and real examples which can be used as the basis for discussion in supervisory training programmes.
- Providing reading assignments of well chosen material with the accompaning instruction to report back, commencing with the words. 'From my reading of this material I consider the following points relevant to my function ...'
- To avoid always focusing on the differences between environmental situations it can be useful to pose an issue in terms of 'this is the situation, problem, solution, method, that is used in a number of countries. Are there any similarities in this environment?'

Other in-course aids to involvement can be:

- providing responsibility by allocating a camera and requesting one of the participants to record the blackboard and flip chart notes;
- delegating responsibility for certain course organising responsibilities;
- encouraging small group discussion leaders to use transparencies for their group reporting;
- assigning summarising responsibilities at the completion of each segment of a programme.

Generally it is true that any situation that can be work-related, localised and participative is worth trying.[7] There

---

7 As a further localising example, a combined role-play and case study is provided in Appendix VI, p. 200.

are risks but the great advantages of working with people in emerging countries are the lack of embarrassment once learning commences and the sincere interest in learning that can be aroused. Learning is serious but it can also have an element of enjoyment.

For senior staff

The term as it is used here is intended to cover all those staff who through their education, their training and development, or through their experience have already reached positions of influence over either events or people.

While the variety of levels of attainment in terms of management knowledge and application is enormous the common denominator within this total group is the ability to absorb new thinking. Attention span will vary; some will be naturally and culturally exuberant; some will be – equally naturally – reserved and careful about self-exposure; some will respond openly while others will wait; but in almost all cases there is a latent interest in self-development.

In adding further to this generalisation an additional associated strength of this widely divergent group is the willingness to devote effort to new ideas and new concepts.

Just as it can be a grave mistake to overestimate level and to assume too much existing knowledge, it can be equally dangerous to underestimate potential. In many of the emerging countries, the 'senior staff' includes graduates from the best universities from both the East and the West. Many of the people are as widely read as their colleagues anywhere in the world and the large majority are at least aware of the forces at work in their own cultures and of the growth potential of their countries. Almost without exception they have the capacity to be coldly critical of anything other than genuine effort.

The ingredients that are often missing are opportunities to fulfil potential, to grow through guided and structured development and experience, and to develop the ability to use knowledge by converting it into action. The last of these factors is in many ways central to the first two as having that knowledge does sometimes tend to become confused with the ability to make use of it. For this reason many of the programmes developed specifically for senior staff tend to resemble the action of finally climbing on the horse. Certainly no amount of instruction regarding the techniques, methods, systems and theories of horse-back riding will prevent the ultimate embarrassment of being thrown to the dust if the ability to perform is not present.

Some practical examples of methods, in addition to those described in the previous sector under the heading of 'highly structured and open ended', and which can have particular relevance for senior staff, are given below. Again, though, because of the divergence of knowledge opportunities, the approaches have to some extent been generalised:

- Joint establishment of goals through training and development programmes similar to that exampled for supervisors. In this case an element of counselling is added and assistance given with the formation of the goals so that the presentation to the senior management can be better prepared and presented.
- Structured recognition of self-development needs through open-ended discussion under the headings of 'in-company climate' and 'profile characteristics of the company'. In all cases where this has been done the consistently emerging pattern has been the desire for more influence in the decision-making process. Such a desire can reflect the fact that in some cases decisions are taken too far away from those with more intimate knowledge of the problems but the self-development side of this coin is again the requirement for improved skills in report writing and in presenting facts.
- The use of exposure to conceptual approaches that are in advance of current needs – used in this case as a declared means of providing tools for thinking. As an example here, the whole concept of management by objectives when presented under the heading of 'An appreciation of ...' can provide tools for thought that can result in a greater attention to target-setting and standards of performance.

- The provision of selected reading materials is a simple means of directing self-development effort. Such an approach works best when there is some selection possibility for the recipients and it is doubtful whether the mere sending out of such material would be of great benefit.
- Utilisation of the 'seasonal' occasions within the normal business schedule. In this way the whole budgeting and forecasting process can not only be made more meaningful by careful explanation of the purpose and the process but it will also become a more effective exercise.
- Involvement in structuring the training and development programmes for those in lower levels can be an ideal means of creating greater self-awareness. This can be achieved by the formation of committees, task groups, etc., who are charged with the responsibility to recommend regarding requirements and at the same time are requested to involve themselves in the execution aspect of making their suggestions a reality.
- Making use of business games and simulations structured as rehearsals for assuming greater responsibility. When used in this way these aids can contribute to self-image development and the responsibility areas of those in the next highest levels can be underlined.

These examples illustrate the point that development is not only concerned with attending courses. The further point must also be made that for this level of staff one of the key ingredients for development is the counselling they receive from their supervisors. In this case the term is used in its broadest sense and is intended to convey the thought that senior managers should use every conceivable method to coach, develop, encourage initiative, support, advise and at all times reinforce the concepts of both responsibility and accountability.

Another approach is to expose the senior staff by paying them the greatest of all compliments – that is, asking for their opinions. To be really meaningful such an exercise should have a practical purpose, should be firmly structured, and there must be an element of feedback. As an example here such an approach can be used as an integral part of determining training and development needs and a form structured for this purpose is provided as Table 3.17. Clearly, participation in such an exercise is in itself a learning experience. Further key points relating to this type of approach are that it should be open-ended and planned in such a way that the follow-up of the exercise is pre-programmed. In other words something must be seen to happen as a result of obtaining the opinions.

This aspect of follow-up is itself a major issue in any training and development activity but is particularly important for senior staff as they are usually very well aware of the importance of the concept in the execution of their own functions. The obvious example here is the man who has been sent to a training course, whether for functional or for development purposes, and returns, possibly from an extensive overseas journey, to find that not only is there the traditional resistance to his new approaches but there is also an apparent lack of interest in what he has learned and been exposed to. Again development of staff at any level in any emerging country is first and foremost a matter of example. Certainly example setting can be a demanding responsibility and often it must be a deliberate process but, in all matters as fundamental as follow up, it can be the ultimate source of motivation and, when neglected, demotivation.

As was mentioned many of the points made in this section have been deliberately generalised. In order to again return to the fact of the differences two examples are taken from countries as far apart as Kenya and Korea. In similar exercises in these two locations the key motivating factors for senior staff were described respectively as being: opportunity to exercise initiative, mutual loyalty, vision, drive, and impartiality; and a climate of mutual trust, respect for local customs, recognition, real authority and consultation. In neither case could the exercise be called a penetrating study but when considering senior staff development it is only practical to be aware of the shades and difference between countries.

Table 3.17 Needs analysis: sample question and action sheets.

QUESTION SHEET *(for one-hour structured discussion)*

Name:.. Location:..............................
Current job title:...
Organisational relationships: ....
....
Key result areas of current job:...
....
....
Other job responsibilities:..
....
....
....
....
Level of contacts inside and outside the company: ....
....
....
....
Definition of own strengths: ....
....
....
Definition of own training requirements:....................................
....
....
....
Ideas regarding increasing job effectiveness: ....
....
....
....
....
....

Table 3.17 continued

QUESTION SHEET – continued

Opinion of general training needs within the company:...............
....
....
....
....
....

General training needs within own department: ....
....
....
....
....
....
....

Specific training needs for own staff: ....
....
....
....
....
....
....

Check on own training requirements: ....
....
....
....
....
....
....

Other comments: ....
....
....
....
....
....
....

Table 3.17 continued

COMMENT SHEET

Name: .... Location: ....
General: .... Personal: ....
....
....
....
....
....
....
....
....
....
....
Action to be taken:
Short-term: ....
....
....
....
....
....
....
....
....
....

Long-term: ....
....
....
....
....
....
....
....
....
....

The demands of reality

It is important when considering the various practical aspects to acknowledge one of the basic realities. Sheer growth, with its initial and on-going demands, can absorb total attention to such a degree that the whole field of people development becomes secondary. What tends to happen in fact is that attention to development is restricted to brief induction and on-the-job skills training. The result in the long run is inevitably that the effort that has been deferred has suddenly to be accelerated.

It is all too easy to criticise such a situation and in those cases when the transfer of a technology is a major issue such a criticism can have real validity. However, criticism of the reality is only useful if it is accompanied by solutions and in this regard there are a number of points that are relevant:

- Ensuring that those responsible for on-the-job training are in fact equipped with the necessary skills. The frequently encountered alternatives include appointment of the oldest, the longest-serving, the least busy, or the newest arrival, as the person responsible.
- Providing where possible a skills school equipped with the appropriate jigs, tools and best benches so that a semblance of off-the-job training can be made supportive to the efforts on the job. Such a skill school could be situated in an unused corner of a new factory or, from known examples, could equally well be placed in a farmhouse that was once the focal point of the factory property.
- Approaching delegation as a progressive learning process. This applies particularly to senior staff where the intention should be to progressively provide a larger share of responsibility. Clearly such responsibility would have to be accompanied by an equal feeling of accountability and structured feed-back.
- Creating an awareness of the fact that planned approaches should be introduced at the first opportunity and, at the same time, ensuring that even without such a formalised plan there is an awareness

of the approaches that have been outlined in the preceding pages. Certainly not all sections of a project will be advancing at the same rate, so that some will have more time than others to introduce the aspect of developing people according to a plan.

If attention is given to such steps it is likely that the planned phase will more easily be introduced. As is always the case in such matters simple efficiency in terms of resource utilisation makes it inevitable that the investment in people development must be made.

Conclusion

- Training and development is likely to be most effective when it is projected within a planned approach.
- An example of such a plan is to use the three phases of: language, which concentrates initial attention on obtaining a common understanding of the words, expressions, and abbreviations in daily usage; of function or skills training, which focuses attention on the technical aspect of tasks in terms of process, procedures and methods; and, the managing phase which is concerned with conveying the various conceptual aspects of management.
- Such a plan can be sufficiently flexible to allow for the 'need to know' aspects and the environmental and time constraints.
- To be fully dynamic the plan should also proceed through the stage of learning to understand the process of change to the stage of learning how to influence change.
- To ensure the appropriate direction and level of learning, the inputs can be given a structured approach. At the same time the learning can be localised by ensuring that the discussion is well guided and open-ended.
- Such an approach can provide a basis on which to build a resource data bank on set subjects. In turn the data bank can be directed towards the various levels of need.

- The localising of the content can open the way for rather free and frank discussions of otherwise emotive issues and at the same time can be a major aid to understanding.
- In structuring programmes for senior staff one of the most important aspects is the provision of opportunities to convert knowledge into action. Example-setting, counselling, exposing opinions and follow-up are four of the vehicles which can be used for this purpose.
- In situations of rapid growth the planned and environment-related approaches must be maintained as objectives.

4 Implications

Selection – the basic implication

'The selection of the most suitably qualified staff of appropriate level and potential' is a phrase so immediately apparent that it can be too quickly passed over – but indeed, it is the central point.

Read many years ago, very often quoted – but from a long-forgotten source – one of the most fundamental and significant statements concerning people development is this:

> Since neither employment nor promotion change a person's fundamental character it follows that the interviewing process has a greater effect on overall motivation and productivity than any other single management act.

Here again, many of the aspects of interviewing and selection, that are so familiar to those trained in the skills, can constitute new learning to those in the emerging countries who are faced with the task of staffing a new activity. The old adage which states the responsibility and investment content of selection by comparing the lifetime salary of one middle-level employee with the cost of purchasing a piece of equipment, is only 'old' to those who have heard it before; similarly, the cost of labour turnover in terms of lost induction and training expenses still comes as a shock sometimes even to those with many years of experience.

For those familiar with the total selection process, the limitations of the employment interview are well known but in the context of the urgent demands imposed by rapid development even these are enlarged:

- *The tendency to overlook essentials.*

  Here the dangers are of enormous proportions and can include the assumption that certain dexterity skills can be taught, that a previously slower-moving environment will automatically mean that people will have the patience to sit for hours on end – perhaps peering through a microscope – and at the same time suddenly develop the skill to assemble miniature pieces of equipment. Without sufficient prior environmental knowledge it is also possible to overlook, for example, the frequently occurring requirement to balance racial or tribal distributions within a work force.

- *The stereotyping or halo effect.*

  If not carefully supervised the same school, college, university, or sub-racial or locational grouping as the interviewer can be the single main contributor to the decision to employ.

- *The tendency to see what you want to see.*

  Sheer desperation to find the required number of people of the required level of skill can turn technicians into engineers, can transform a typist into a secretary, can derive potential from mediocrity and can lead to ultimate disaster.

- *Over-emphasis on manner and appearance.*

  'Smoothness' is a universal characteristic – not restricted to the 'developed' countries. 'Clothes maketh the man' is best translated into clothes can make an effective man look effective – but they can't convert the appearance of effectiveness into effective performance.

- *The convenience of easy communication in the English language.*

  Contrary to the opinion held by most speakers of the English language this is not necessarily the ultimate indication of superior intelligence – in fact the element of convenience in this regard has, is, and will cause more employment mistakes to be made than any other single factor. The ability to speak English is not an implicit indicator of engineering, accounting, negotiating or any other skill. The willingness to make the effort to learn English or any other language can on the other hand be a necessary qualification for any otherwise very good engineer or accountant.

Nevertheless when the need is great and time is short the employment interview is the most readily available method of selection.

The vital significance of selection as an element of people development makes it imperative to dwell, at least in brief, on some of the fundamentals that may prove helpful in the training of the people who will have any involvement in this task. Some of the familiar key points are:

- At most levels the employment interview is a twenty- to forty-minute encounter between two people – that can change the entire life of a man and his family.
- Because it involves people the interview potentially involves emotions. In the briefest terms it is a socially acceptable method of assessment with the principal purpose of reducing the possibility of failure on both sides.
- Again, because it involves people it creates a relationship and such a relationship can be both revealing and positive only if there are sufficient points of real conversational contact. The responsibility for creating these points of contact rests with the interviewer. The fact that the contact involves emotions also means that insincerities on either side will be easily exposed.
- In developing situations many people are usually engaged to be trained and to work in groups. In such a situation group interaction and cohesion can be an important factor for developing the potential of individuals in the group. Again, this is an another reason for patience and care both when interviewing and, later, when forming sub-groups and working units.

The objective when selecting and placing new employees is always to ensure that, as far as it is possible to forecast, they are put into situations where they have a fair chance of being successful and, at the same time, a precalculated and fair chance of being well adjusted within their work group and working environment.

When this objective is seen as a practical problem, three main points emerge:

- First, it is necessary to discover what human qualities are likely to make for success or failure in any position.
- Second, is the skill to be able to discover these qualities – and the patience to keep looking for them. In the emerging countries this is a matter of being able to recognise potential at every level of employment.
- Third, and implicit, is the neccesity to have a method for comparing the detailed knowledge of the required human qualities with any given set of human characteristics.

With its demands on both objectivity and self-discipline this whole process is difficult and fragile enough in any country, but in an emerging country these difficulties are compounded by language and cultural factors – not to repeat the points made in Chapter 1 regarding management-style expectations and employing company philosophies.

Here it is a matter of giving the interviewer the tools to

Table 4.1 The interviewer's basic job knowledge

The interviewer's basic job knowledge must include:

(a) Knowledge of each job function to the extent that he can verbalise[1] it as a working whole.

(b) Knowledge of the particular work process to the extent that he can verbalise each job's interrelationship.

(c) Knowledge of the working environment so that he can verbalise it to the extent that there will be no later disillusionment.

---

[1] The word 'verbalise' is used here as a training device to encourage development of the skill in a learning situation.

perform his expected task and the outline set out as Tables 4.1, 4.2 and 4.3 is an example of a pre-interviewing guide that has been prepared for this purpose from standard material and used in a number of countries.[2]

In many instances the man being trained and developed to conduct the interviewing will be asked to do so against the background of absolutely no prior experience. In some situations he will also be requested to recruit people for situations that do not at that time exist – except in a near-completion or final building stage.

As a word of caution it is important to note that the concept of job descriptions should be handled with great care.[3] The temptation is to prepare these documents in fine detail in order to make the setting-up stage more predictable. While this approach has undoubted value for certain types of work the impression of rigidity in the more

Table 4.2   The interviewer's detailed knowledge

The interviewer's detailed knowledge must include:

Skill demands

- Required immediate level of mental capacity in terms of both difficulty and speed as well as accuracy.

- Required level of muscular skill in terms of both short-term and longer-duration time spans.

- Required level of spatial and visual ability with regard to shapes, size and colour or any other specific value.

- Required level of precision in terms of measurement or placement.

- Other skill demands.

---

2 For a further example of standard material under this heading also see p. 120.

3 An earlier comment is provided on p. 24 and the point is further illustrated on p. 162.

Table 4.2 continued

Equipment, tools and materials

- Information regarding the tools to be used and their uses.

- Information regarding the nature of the material to be handled.

- Information regarding the machinery or equipment that either form part of the work process or are part of the working environment.

- Information regarding specific clothing or dress in terms of both requirements and restrictions.

- Other relevant information.

Job characteristics

- Description of the current and planned working conditions.

- Description of the composition of the work group in terms of numbers, location and growth.

- Description of the social contact opportunities; for example, for conversation within the work group.

- Other job characteristics.

Training available

- Individual or group learning situations.

- Duration of learning situations.

- Achievement levels and criteria for success.

- Types of learning opportunities that become available once the first set of criteria have been satisfied.

Table 4.2 continued

Conditions of employment

- Criteria for payment.
- Pay scale, structure and progression.
- Hours of work and explanation of any differences.
- Amenities, including any subsidy details.
- Transportation possibilities and cost.
- Accommodation, including cost and subsidy information.
- Leave and when due.
- Benefits that exist or are planned.
- Other social or welfare benefits.

---

senior levels has to be avoided. The positive reasons for this fact are that flexibility will support the growth of initiative, will create a more dynamic working climate, will encourage joint efforts and will underline achievement as the central issue. The negative reasons in this case are of equal importance. Disciplined job descriptions can too readily be interpreted as boxes that confine responsibility and promote the growth of upward delegation of both authority and responsibility. At their worst such job descriptions can also be used as convenient excuses for under-performance.

The practical solution here is to create job responsibility areas that are open-ended but subject to pre-discussed levels of achievement. The critical ingredient is not so much the written description as the pre-discussion and performance dialogue. In this way the paper work becomes a supportive aid to effective performance.

Two further cautionary comments are largely self-explanatory. First, it is vital to be honest enough to recognise that some applicants will be too over-qualified. To employ them in the hope that they can be satisfied can be self-defeating as news of disappointment travels quickly in these countries – and in the same manner turnover of key staff can spread like a disease. The second cautionary remark concerns the temptation to over-pay the 'man we

Table 4.3 Information to be obtained or confirmed

- Education.
- Experience.
- Knowledge gained.
- Why job changes occurred, if any.
- Current family circumstances.
- Current financial circumstances.
- Why interested in position being discussed.
- Health.
- Probable reaction to supervision.
- Potential for retention.
- Potential for greater responsibilities.
- Examples of previous initiative.
- Enthusiasms.
- Limitations for any reason related to the skill demands, the equipment, tools and materials demands, or job characteristics.
- Any other limitations.

can't do without'. The price of upsetting a payment structure may sometimes far exceed the inconvenience of taking more time or investing more effort in developing another man.

To return to the practical problem of familiarising both the people responsible for interviewing and those responsible for selection with the realities, the suggestion is to use the readily available technique of role playing. The actual application of the method will depend on the attitudes existing in a particular environment. In some cases people will be nervous and time will be required in order to create a relaxed learning atmosphere; in other cases the atmosphere will be one of exuberance, high spirits and rare acting talent. While there will be locations where the role playing should exclude cases that can cause embarrassment through association with imagined known situations, the two examples set out as Tables 4.4 and 4.5 were used in a country where recognisable reality is the best means of creating a meaningful learning situation. The first example is a standard ice-breaker were both the role players and the audience can concentrate on technique. The second is totally environment-related.

Those organisations who seek only to buy or bargain for talent will find that the resources may be limited. In many cases the skills simply do not exist. In others, the process of bargaining for a related skill or ability can only be at the cost of the company or institution that made the initial development effort and investment. This limited talent resource can result from the wide variety of factors generally including sub-standard schooling, a background of predominantly short-term goals, and in certain countries, from a general lassitude which can derive from generations of acceptance of a declining quality of life.
There are several practical issues here:

- *The need to become familiar with whatever talent resources are available.*

  Depending on the political and social circumstances there may be small sub-groups who possess talents above the norm. Of these the military is often the most likely talent source and in many cases it has been shown that military training can make a more or less immediate contribution. Often such people are familiar with some type of discipline, have some skill training and know something of the problems of supply and maintenance.

- *The need to know and understand the attitudes to education.*

  In many cases those young men who have studied abroad see their years in American or European universities either as a fulfilled end-goal or as an entry into further security in government service. This is certainly not always the case but it is something to be aware of.

- *The need to look closely at the infrastructure.*

  There is always some systematic approach to education. It can be through either church or state and the basic enthusiasm for learning can usually be found in the high schools. It is in this area where immediate relationships can be developed in terms of mutual aid and assistance.

Table 4.4   Interviewing role play I: Standard

---

1 *Facts about the applicant* (This information to be given to the interviewee.)
- Age 36
- Married, 2 children
- Renting a house
- Achieved officer rank during his military training.
- Motor mechanic
- Ran country garage for a period of six months employing small staff.
- Feels that he has a grasp of routine business operations.
- Has applied for a position as a supervisor.
- Interests are largely mechanical but is a member of the public relations committee of his local rotary group.
- Is concerned that he may be too old and does not fully understand the requirement for one year's training in electronics. Is also uncertain regarding the need to transfer to another factory but would be prepared to face this need if he felt it worthwhile.
- This man is a most acceptable candidate for a supervisory position in a social and personal sense.

2 *Facts known by the interviewer about the applicant* (This information to be given to the interviewer.)
- Age 36
- Married, 2 children
- Motor mechanic
- Applicant has mechanical interests.
- Applicant is a member of the public relations committee of some local association.

3 *Facts which the interviewer particularly wants to check*
- Applicant's supervisory potential.
- Applicant's preparedness to study practical electronics.
- Applicant's preparedness to accept transfer.

Table 4.5   Interviewing role play II: Environment-related

1 *Facts about the applicant* (This information to be given to the interviewee)
   - Age 42
   - Married with 4 children at school
   - Living in appropriate location
   - Military school—Electronic Communications.
   - Army signal corps 6 years.
   - Supply forces factory making electronic parts for communications equipment for 3 years.
   - Staff warehousing function 6 years.
   - Teaching junior school 3 years.
   - Enthusiastic to get back into industry.

2 *Facts known by the interviewer about the applicant* (This information to be given to the interviewer.)
   - Age 42
   - Married
   - Has academic qualification
   - Some industrial experience
   - Man is enthusiastic

3 *Facts which interviewer wants to check*
   - Check experience
   - Check current knowledge
   - Must find out sufficient information to enable him to make a decision whether or not to arrange for a second interview.

Note: The realistic key point in this case is to determine whether or not the applicant has retained sufficient of his engineering knowledge to enable him to be employed as a factory engineer at a managing level—what did he do in the signal corps; what were his responsibilities in the supply forces; what is the validity of 6 years warehousing experience and 3 years of school teaching—can he—and does he now have the knowledge to start a new life?

- *The need to remember the familiar tools and techniques.*
  For people requiring the basic manipulative skills,
  tests can easily be revised to suit local circumstances.
  In fact local artists can readily be engaged to redraw
  the diagrams and such a step can only help the total
  integration.
- *The need to devise new approaches.*
  The interviewing process described earlier can be
  given a new dimension by further extension into the
  area of potential. Questions relating to growth,
  awareness of priorities, knowledge of local culture,
  understanding of the need for continuity of learning,
  all become factors to be considered. As has also been
  indicated, the traditional job description preparation
  for the interviewing of middle- and senior-level staff
  can also be the initial phase in establishing the criteria
  for the later assessment of actual performance.
- *The need to communicate.*
  Ensure understanding by defining requirements and
  assessing potential in local terms. In all countries
  communication is only possible through understanding.
- *The need to use the experience of others.*
  When in doubt look for others with experience and
  find the success stories. Perhaps the best short cut is to
  interview successful local people and to discover the
  key factors in their approaches and values. This
  provides an initial point of reference that can save
  hours of otherwise wasted time.
- *The need to remain realistic.*
  The fact that there may not be a pool of people with
  appropriate talents is no reflection on the abilities of a
  group of people. Experience in many countries has
  demonstrated that when the element of opportunity is
  provided, both the learning and the performance can
  far exceed the expectations.

It is important under this heading to look briefly at the
concept of motivation. While the idea that work itself,
through recognition and self-fulfilment, can be a source of
satisfaction is well enough accepted in many countries,
there are other countries where the concept has to be seen

from quite a different perspective. Calorie intake and malnutrition can create a situation where the focal point of life can be survival itself. Job satisfaction can be concerned with the simple fact of having a job rather than with the nature of the work.

Training – the reality

While 'training' as a word is in danger of becoming an imagined panacea, training as a concept has to be seen in relation to the need, the value and the return on investment. Further, it has to be seen in a particular context and as part of a package which includes the determination of organisational goals, the selection of suitably qualified staff of appropriate potential, the development of effective organisation structures and the implementation of motivating aids through performance feed-back and salary systems.

In cost-benefit terms, training must be supportive to the organisational and business requirements. In general management terms, all managers need to be sufficiently knowledgeable to be able to formulate reasonable expectations and to make realistic demands on those responsible for training implementation. Further, they need to be aware of the importance of their own roles in this process. Included in these inescapable roles are such aspects as example-setting, attention to the quality of their order-giving, their development of task-setting approaches, demonstrations of interest in work progress and their skill in counselling.

Against this background the training concept can be better seen within the total dynamic framework of organisation and business reality.

From this point of view it is a per country, per organisation matter to fill in the details but the guiding headings can readily be established. By utilising what has been described in the preceding pages these headings could be presented as:

- needs per skill area – current and projected
- needs per function area – current and projected

- needs for knowledge – current and projected
- envisioned needs for the future
- resources per skill area
- resources per function area
- knowledge-centred resources

While the headings may be brief the lists they lead to can be both elaborate and fairly comprehensive. The complementary components here are the specification of individual as well as group needs, the organisation level of needs, and research of the quality of in-company, in-country and third party resources.

The need to plan – the second implication

One of the critical requirements in the whole area of people development is planning. This applies to all aspects of the employment of people but, without detracting from the importance of manpower scheduling and the other employment-related techniques, the intention here is to concentrate on the vital aspect of management and career-development planning. This is the element that is of greatest significance in the emerging countries. It is important both to employing organisations and to governments, as it is the most practical vehicle for exposing talent, for selective development and for displaying the efforts and investments that are made and the results that are achieved in this total field.

Once again it is a process with each part being vital to the fulfilment of the whole. Being part of standard management practice there are countless theories, but the information presented here is derived from an experience in a particular country which has since been developed as a resource system and been subject to several application variations.

The essence of the approach is the dynamism of each of the component parts and therefore of the total process. The other essential ingredients are that it is relatively simple both to apply and to explain to those who are involved; it is at all times related to the purpose of the enterprise; it provides planned replacement schedules and it is entirely flexible without losing its basic objective. It is not intended as a discipline nor as a system confined to board room considerations. It is both a tool and a part of the total learning process.

The components of the process are:
- dynamic organisation charting
- performance assessment
- individual assessment and development planning
- inventorisation of individual assessments and needs
- management development planning
- career and succession planning.

For reasons of clarity and in order to further illustrate the example each of the above components is examined as a separate entity.

Dynamic organisation charting

Here, the word 'dynamic' is used deliberately to avoid any association with the concept of the static charting of how a particular organisation looked yesterday. The concept in this case is to view the organisation as an on-going network which is structured for growth.

The practical objective is to picture the organisation in terms of both positions and people, and the achievement of this objective is only possible through the association of the current and projected business reality with the organisation and people realities. In addition fulfilment of the objective is fully dependent on the degree of interaction and involvement that can be built up among the senior staff. Seen in this way not only the charting is dynamic, but also the process of charting is itself entirely active, participative and developmental.

The actual presentation of such a chart will depend to a large extent on the particular organisation or company involved but again, for the sake of example, the illustration provided as Figure 4.1 is based on an actual case and has been generalised in terms of job titles only in order to make it more generally useful.

Clearly, when seen on an organisation-wide basis such a chart will take on another order of complexity and names will be seen to be interchangeable between departments.

Figure 4.1 Dynamic organisation charting

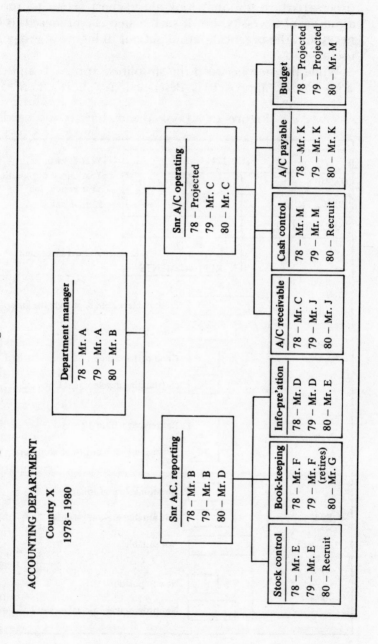

Clearly also, it is a short step from this relatively simple process to the traditional 'look-ahead chart'. Here it is more a matter of necessity, but if such a step is considered to be necessary, the practical outline set out in Figure 4.2 may be useful.

While the step between the simplified approach and the 'look-ahead' approach is described as 'short' there are

Figure 4.2   Look-ahead chart

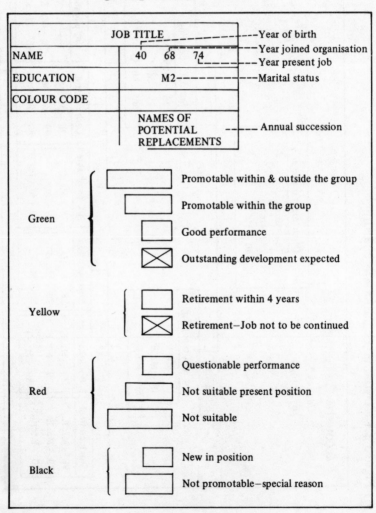

major differences – the purpose of the first approach can, for immediately pratical purposes, be achieved through dynamic discussion, but the second approach contains the implication of a more formalised approach to people assessment.

Performance assessment

Once again the number of approaches that have been designed for this purpose are endless and as the type of system will depend very much on on-going or preconceived ideas it is not the intention to present any single ideal solution.

A suggestion regarding this matter is however contained in the section dealing with job descriptions under the heading 'Selection'. The point made there referred to the establishment of job responsibility areas and the essential ingredients of such an approach are that:[4]

- assessment of performance takes place against the main achievement areas of any given position;
- there is pre-discussion between the man making the assessment and the man being assessed;
- the pre-discussion is concerned with the performance level that will be expected and that is believed by both parties to be achievable;
- the pre-discussion contains guidance and at the same time provides for flexibility of both method and approach;
- the pre-discussion takes into account the fact that other tasks, apart from the main achievement tasks, will have to be performed;
- there is an understanding reached regarding feed-back concerning difficulties that may be encountered in regard to both the task itself and the pre-discussed time for its fulfilment;
- there is agreement reached concerning the criteria for later assessment, the method of progress reporting and the ultimate fact that achievement will be one of

4 The earlier reference appears on pp. 93 and 96 and the concept is illustrated on p. 162.

the determining factors in measuring success and in determining compensation.

Necessarily in such a system there is a need to record expectations and to formulate those expectations into what can become a useful means of recording effective performance. This is of course not in any respect an end in itself nor does it in any way replace the normal daily contact or counselling occasions. It is however a useful, structured and dynamic means of placing emphasis on the importance of interaction. The responsibility for ensuring that the pre-discussion is indeed a pre-'discussion' rests with the man in the role of potential assessor and the occasion itself should be regarded as a medium for both training and development.

There is a clear relationship with the 'management by objectives' method but the approach suggested here is as much designed for training and development purposes as it is for assessment. In terms of the earlier requirements it is desophisticated to the extent that it is communicable and it retains its end purpose.

Individual assessment and development planning

The purpose under this heading is to consider the level of performance achievement in terms of the needs for development. It will be apparent that this approach to analysing training needs does not replace the normal predictive methods – rather, it is an important supplementary aid.

Clearly from the level of achievement it will be possible to consider those factors that have been inhibiting. As was mentioned earlier these can be conveniently catagorised under the headings of skills needs, functional needs and knowledge needs. Similarly they may relate to attitude and personality factors. The distinct advantage here is that, when seen against the background of actual performance, the emerging needs can pave the way for non-emotive counselling.

Given the added ingredient of dynamic organisation charting, both the analysis of needs and the counselling become dynamic, reality-based and totally environment-related – three of the fundamental criteria for effective action in the emerging countries. The theoretical concepts are at the same time retained and a base for later sophistication is firmly grounded in the normal supportive approaches to the business.

Inventorisation of individual assessments and needs

Here we are concerned with the total structuring of the required actions in terms of

- organisation planning from the dynamic organisation charting
- predicted personal development requirements based on regular observation and longer-term envisioned planning
- development-gap considerations arising from levels of achievement when seen against expectations
- the results of regular counselling in terms of the self-declared aspirations of those under review.

When seen in this way it is possible to design a matrix of names and needs under headings which are abbreviations of the four points mentioned above. At the same time the list illustrated under the earlier heading of 'Training' can then be expanded as in Table 4.6.

Table 4.6   Skills, functions and knowledge requirements[5]

	Organisation planning	Observed prediction	Achievement gap	Aspiration	Comment regarding priorities & timing
Name					
Name					
Name					
Name					
Name					
Name					

5 An earlier reference is made on p. 21 and the concept is further illustrated on pp. 163–4.

Through this simplified illustration it is intended both to underline the need for structure and to evidence the total dynamics of the process. Priorities and timing are matters for discussion and interaction and once again the planned approach has the advantage that it can be used as evidence of understanding of a local growth situation.

Management development planning

In this case emphasis is placed on resources – both in terms of people and in terms of solutions to the revealed needs – and on potential.

The positive people resources can be projected as promotables; their movement within the organisation network can be given a wider vision and successors can be prepared.

The requirement for resources to satisfy the training and development needs can be given structure and investigation of those resources can be directed towards both the business and the people realities.

In the emerging country context this search for resources can include in-company, in-country and international investigations. This point has been mentioned earlier and will be further reviewed in regard to total national development.[6] The key point however is that when the total approach is structured in the manner outlined above the costs of development can be better recognised as investments in the future.

Because such an approach is dynamic it is implicit that it will also have multidirectional consequences. In this regard, in addition to revealing the development requirements of potential successors, it will reveal the potential demand for replacements at all levels. Again, this point will be further reviewed when considering the essential relationship between companies and the host country.

Career and succession planning

On the basis of the collective inputs it is possible to develop

---

6 See also p. 122 and the elaboration and illustration on pp. 157 and 158.

a living picture that combines the business reality, the people, and the future. It is further possible to incorporate in such a picture future intentions regarding an in-company expatriate population of whatever size. Where necessary the impracticability of replacing such an expatriate population can also be evidenced.

The matrix chart presented in outline in Figure 4.3 can be as simplified or as complex as is necessary to meet the demands of the organisation. It can be prepared for internal use only or, where required, can be prepared for presentation to any concerned government.

In this case the chart has been designed to show the purpose of the exercise and some further explanatory notes may be helpful:

- The information on the left hand side of the chart can be extended to include age, years of service, and job grading where such a system is in operation.
- The top portion can also be similarly extended by the job grade feature as this will be useful in order to further indicate both job grade and career advancement.
- The intersecting squares where name and position correspond can be used to indicate potential for mobility.
- By the addition of a simple colour code with each colour representing one each of a number of years the whole chart can be converted into a dynamic statement. For example, it is predictable that over the course of a number of years one man may be seen to have possibilities for a number of positions. Similarly a number of people may be seen to have possibilities for the same position.
- The squares containing the mobility factor can be treated in the same way so that each square may potentially contain a coloured cross to indicate the year when that person will be considered ready for transfer or promotion, or for training that may involve absence from his position for an extended period.
- Those with no potential for mobility will be immediately identifiable by the absence of any marking.

Figure 4.3   Career and succession planning

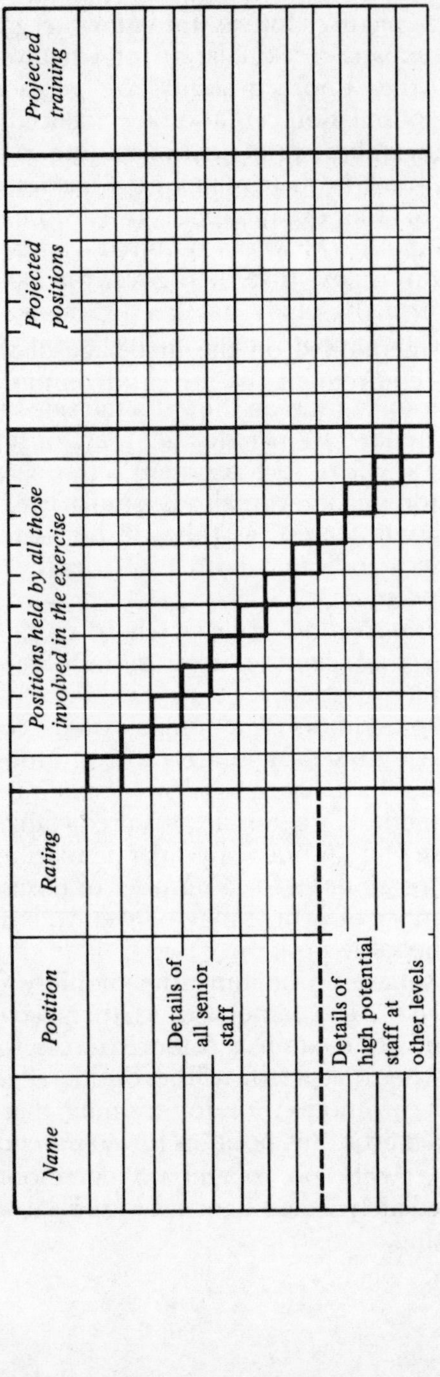

Name	Position	Rating	Positions held by all those involved in the exercise	Projected positions	Projected training
	Details of all senior staff				
	Details of high potential staff at other levels				

- The movement of high-potential staff into the senior staff sector, and the total movement into the area of projected positions, will indicate potential vacancies long before they become crisis problems. In this way determined recruitment efforts can be planned well in advance.
- The inclusion of expatriate staff in the senior staff sector will immediately identify whether or not their replacement is being planned, and, similarly the completion of the projected training section will indicate the efforts that are being made to prepare their replacements.

As was mentioned on the first page of this section the essential requirement is for a dynamic and planned approach to training and development which is appropriate to the current and future needs of both the purpose of the organisation and the people in it.

Another element mentioned earlier, which can be a vital factor in the approach developed in the immediately preceding pages, is the possibility of using accepted management aids and support systems for the added purpose of people development. The critical elements to be developed are the involvement of, and the interaction between, people. This approach is further developed in the next two sections, which deal briefly with the subjects of planned personnel strategy and the planned introduction of policy.

Pre-planning of personnel strategy

In any organisation the personnel function can be directed either as an agent of continuity or as an agent of structured change. While the personality and character of the men responsible for that function are always important considerations the fact remains that in a situation of change the most able men will not be able to perform or exercise initiative without a well-guided set of directions. In an emerging country the whole environment is tuned to change and the elements of direction and structure are vital. In such a situation the alternative to structure is the temptation to spread effort in all directions and the only result can be chaos.

As was stated in an earlier section the key points are knowledge of local law, knowledge of local practice and awareness of the usual norms of the organisation.[7] The more involvement there is in the creation of the structured approach the more commitment there will be to its fulfilment.

Again a practical example may best serve to illustrate the point. In this case the example comes from a country where there has been a 300 per cent increase in activity in three years and where well-co-ordinated government relationships are essential. The environment in this case had developed to the point where, because of the growth-based political confidence, the social regulations in the country were proceding at a pace which was some years ahead of the real economic growth. In this particular example the purpose of the exercise was to ensure that the approaches were reality-based in terms of all the information available from internal and external sources. After considerable local discussion the personnel strategy statement read as follows:

To identify the role of the personnel department with the business and people needs of the organisation, the essential priorities in the personnel sector are as follows:

1 Recruitment on the basis of planned manpower requirements.
2 Objective, qualitative and quantitative assessment of the existing human resources.
3 Objective assessment of the requirements of the organisation in terms of people development and in terms of support systems.
4 Development of the necessary training and people development programmes.
5 Development of and maintenance of the appropriate employee relations support systems and the establishment of the appropriate routines and guides for action.
6 Establishment of a management information

---

7 See also p. 20.

system relating in particular to reporting regarding relevant legislation.

7 The development of a feedback system of reporting regarding the above priorities so that management is regularly informed of progress and constantly informed of significant trends within the social environment of the country.

The contents of this corporate personnel strategy statement are prepared as a guiding basis for the development of detailed policy planning and as a basis for the development of initiatives in this sector.

While the above priorities have become more sophisticated in the subsequent years and the language has been refined, the essential skeleton of the structure remains.

The main results of such an approach are that the components of management objectives and language, in becoming an inbuilt part of policy, quickly become familiar to all in the organisation. In a further example which is provided in the 'Key points and summarised conclusions', this point is again emphasised in a section dealing with the introduction of the concept of increasing effectiveness through training and development.[8]

This familiarity with management objectives and language not only makes for ease of communication but it also provides a setting in which policy acceptance is more readily achievable. The emphasis on people in terms of planned recruitment, human-resource assessment, planned people-development, employee relations support systems and social environment, together with the specific mention of legislation and significant trends, also demonstrates a set of positive attitudes towards the local circumstances and local progress.

To reinforce the value of this strategic approach it may be of interest to note some of the developments that have taken place since its implementation. These include:

- Quantitative manpower planning – which is sufficiently sophisticated for the local situation and

8 See also pp. 158–64.

which can be developed to meet the growth demands of the organisation.

- Inventorisation of staff – relatively desophisticated but, again, sufficient for the organisation's requirements.
- Appraisal and needs analysis – with the system containing the initial shades of job- and results-related performance assessment and with concentration on needs determination.
- Training and staff development – still in the skills and language phases with some attention to the managing phase.[9]
- Employee relations – policy development which is only converted into statements of policy after careful study of local law and practice.
- Recreation and welfare – utilisation of optimal opportunities for joint occasions using local circumstances to their best advantage.
- Management information system – structured for further development but in accordance with the requirements and ensuring trend awareness.
- Communications – through the language reinforcement and repetition and through regular editions of an informative and social newsletter.
- Community integration – through both local and central government contacts, through the establishment of relationships with high schools and universities and through maintaining an employee resource file which ensures follow-up with previously rejected, but possibly appropriate, job candidates.
- Industry integration – by making proper use of the usual top-level contacts and by taking an initiating role in such aspects as compensation surveys and surveys of local practice.

At all times the development of people is fundamental to the rapid development of the positive working climate that makes this type of implementation possible. As has been mentioned, a key point in this regard is the way in which policy is introduced.

9 For the initial illustration see also p. 50.

Pre-planning of policy announcements

This is one of those cases where the lessons learned in the longer-established organisations can be immediately converted into a practical change of approach. In the emerging organisations both the pre-planning and the implementation of policy can be a means of communication and an aid to development. The introduction of a degree of disciplined thinking into what, in some cases, could have been a relatively unstructured society, without some degree of pre-planning would otherwise in itself be a major problem.

Again the exercise is directed towards involvement and the use of language. The key words here are 'Management/ Supervisory guide'. In brief this is in reality a management manual with the added ingredient of interpretation and application guidance – but the difference between a manual or book of directions and a guide to implementation is critical in terms of both acceptance and development.[10]

For practical reasons it is difficult to provide a complete example in this case but it is possible to illustrate the outline of the concept. For reasons of convenience, which are related to the relative speed of change, such an illustration is best pictured as being part of a loose-leaf binder. Once again this serves to underline the dynamic nature of the environment and the organisation's reaction to change and growth. Further, it has to be seen in the context of the discussions that preceded its presentation – here it is a matter of dignifying people by obtaining their prior opinions – it is a matter of pre-education – it is a matter of creating a 'feeling' of being involved – it is a matter also of a degree of pre-commitment.

Table 4.7 illustrates these points. Simplicity itself? Not really, as it puts the burden on those with the responsibility to inform – through the policy objective – and to educate – through the policy application.

The principal point is the detailing of the role of the responsible supervisor. Here it is a matter of using every possible opportunity to state policy in terms of positives and

---

10 An earlier reference is made on p. 47.

Table 4.7 Management guide outline

MANAGEMENT GUIDE	Policy no.
	Effective date:
	Approved by:

Policy subject:

Policy objective:

Policy statement:

Policy application (detailing the role of the responsible supervisor):

to leave room for discretion. The other end of this reasoning is that in this way supervisors are forced to supervise and forced to be responsible for their decisions within the limits prescribed by the policy. The too frequently encountered alternative is that supervisors are told what not to do and that in cases of doubt they should direct the enquiry to a higher authority. In other words there is an immediate awareness of the limitation of authority, there is always a place to hide and there is always a way in which to avoid healthy confrontation.

In the emerging country context the purpose must always be to develop structured approaches that promote growth and self-development. To minimise responsibility must always result in inhibited growth. Certainly such an approach is unlikely to expose either capacity for initiative or potential for development.

A further reality – problem identification the key step to structured solutions

Selection, training, planning – are all reflections of an ideal, but the reality of growth also needs to be examined from the point of view of the pains of growth. Growing pains produce distortions and, while it may be uncomfortable and perhaps embarrassing, there is nothing to be gained by ignoring the symptoms of those pains – perhaps in fact there is something to be learned by exposing them.

- Through uncertainty, lack of experience and a touch of desire to hold on to and to make apparent the most spectacular symbols of success, there can sometimes be a reluctance to delegate real authority. This tends to produce a situation where, for example, the most expensive people are signing approvals for the most insignificant work. Through the development of a multiplier effect these 'managers' become extremely busy, self-satisfied and secure in their role. The unfortunate result, though, is they become totally unproductive and the younger people have a choice between uncomplaining laziness and bitter frustration.

- Priorities can often appear to be based on the order of events, over a day, a week, a month or a year rather than on the potential organisational impact of problems. While the explanation can sometimes be seen to be related to the agrarian work-cycle the result is that the organisation is jolted from crisis to crisis with the periods of calm becoming shorter and progressively less frequent.

- The most basic organisational principles only appear in that framework through long familiarity, through training and development and through the fact that they become customary. On the other hand in many of the emerging countries, the behaviours implicit in that framework seem to be as unnatural and difficult to learn as a gold stroke. Concepts like matching authority with responsibility, providing opportunities for growth, giving trust to promote honest reactions, recognising that an instruction to act can involve the taking of initiatives beyond the instruction, passing on credit for suggestions made and many more, have to be learned and developed.

- Mistakes will be made in the best-managed organisations; targets will sometimes not be met –

but, as can happen when the experience base is too shallow, when the mistakes are hidden rather than acknowledged and when the missed targets are never reported, the opportunities to recover, to learn from experience and to correct for the future, are lost for ever.

- The process of change and the development of the young are traditionally difficult but these difficulties are severely compounded in a situation where a subordinate suggestion can be regarded as a threat to authority and where the established system is allowed to become a series of loopholes, hiding places for past indiscretions, protective devices for favoured friends and a network of mutually concealed mistrust. In some cases the term 'system' can itself imply the development of a counter-system which consists of ways and means of avoiding – or even defeating – the original intentions.

While it is true that such a list of generalisations could be both longer and more dramatic, the only point in stating them at all is to underline the fact that it would be unrealistic to ignore them. That they can be overcome has been proved often enough but they are only overcome through effort – an effort that can only be effective if it is made with understanding of causes as well as with concern for the effects.

Criticism is not curative and the tools are training, development, education and exampled behaviour.

Problem areas to be overcome

It is also important to acknowledge other problems and negative factors that have to be overcome.

Perhaps the most apparent of these is the factor of 'isation' in the sense of a particular government pressure to impose local people in higher-level positions before they are fully prepared. Training and development and the implementation of the type of succession planning founded on the hard analysis and factual approach that has been described can help to respond to such pressures and should be used to avoid unhealthy antagonisms and conflicts and to aid constructive dialogue with local authorities. When organisations, with the aid of foreign managers, are seen to be developing local people this can only serve to reduce the pressure to remove the foreign managers at faster than the planned rate. Such foreign managers are expensive and one of their tasks in most cases is to develop their own replacements, and certainly by adding a structured vision of organisation growth to that of country growth it can be possible to heighten both internal motivation and government co-operation. It could be foreseen that host country governments will indeed insist on the introduction of the type of structured approach that has been described.

Another common negative factor that has already been mentioned is that which derives from a situation where there may be many new foreign investors in an area and where only a few make any real attempt to develop their people. High labour turnover is the inevitable result with the victims being the organisations making the development effort. Again there can be a temptation to join those who do nothing, but this can only be self defeating. The real solutions are to tailor-make the training effort even more closely to specific organisation requirements and to promote a more widespread development effort.

In fact the development of people cannot take place in isolation. Ideally such an exercise should be a joint activity with industry, government and education authorities taking mutually supporting approaches. Neither can the business-oriented development of people be separated from aspects of social development and general economic progress. Through their business training people can acquire new attitudes to the demands of economic life, can be exposed to the values of organised approaches, can see merit arising from co-operation and place the role of education and learning in new perspective. As needs and resources become more clearly identified so too do the demands for greater opportunity. Clearly, then, the education of managers cannot be a selfish process. It brings with it a social commitment not only to the people who are developed, but also to the people who are influenced by that development. Further, just as an organisation, in recognising common denominators among its high priority needs, may utilise a regional approach to developing its managers, that same organisation could, through finding the same or similar needs in the business, private or public sectors of the internal environment, stimulate joint external approaches. Through intensive co-operation any organisation can contribute to the general infrastructure of a country and can integrate itself within that country's growth process.

Implications for countries

Essentially the difference between organisations and countries is a matter of scale but the principles remain very much the same.

Experience indicates that many of the emerging countries, while fully acknowledging the realities of their own situations, are extremely capable of deriving lessons from the more industrialised countries and of devising new, and often more effective, solutions to their own problems.

Many are able to do this within the context of their four or five-year development plans and, indeed, this is the key point which provides a clear focus on people development as a basic factor of overall resource development. Viewed in such a way, the planning of training and education in the fields of both skills and management is a natural and integral aspect of national planning. Where this degree of recognition of the relevance and interdependance of these factors exists, people development will be synchronised with – and within – the objectives and strategies of the development planning. In such cases education can be undertaken according to a set of priorities and where this is accomplished successfully, investment projects will be aided by the qualitative and quantitative availability of the appropriate people talents.

Clearly the number, diversity, duration and sheer magnitude of needs which will emerge from pre-calculation of the requirements calls for various scenarios and, while the scenario concept is well-enough known in terms of pure economics, it is not so often practised in regard to people. The criteria for such an exercise are in all respects the same as have been detailed previously. Put into country terms, they could be summarised as follows:

- Precalculation of priority needs, according to the alternative economic constructions, in terms of basic and advanced skills and of supervisory, support and management requirements.
- Pre-design of resource structures that will satisfy the priority requirements.
- Rationalisation of both the immediate and short-term priorities against longer-term considerations so that the resultant provision of facilities will be seen as permanent.
- Co-ordination of the available and potential effort of all appropriate agencies and activities that can be used or developed as resources.
- Forecasting of resource gaps within the period of the development plan – together with precalculation of predictable future resource gaps.
- Analysis of requirements for international support on a pre-planned and highly selective basis.

As a result of such a deliberate approach the facts that emerge will be entirely practical and directed towards achievement. The task is of course to make the implementation feasible. All economic sectors and all levels of training and education will at least have been considered. The built-in consideration of priorities will further ensure that the initial investments in this sector will be in accordance with the most urgent needs of the country. The alternative, which is the not unfamiliar *ad hoc* expediency approach, will only serve to endanger and undermine the whole concept of economic planning.

Clearly these priorities are not static measurements and the approach that any country adopts must also ensure that not only are the priorities updated, but also that the changing demands for new levels of knowledge are known in advance. This implies that any country, like any organisation, must have an on-going awareness of its specific people development requirements and that there are continuing plans directed towards knowledge development. This is particularly relevant when the speed of change is the predominant factor.

The further implication that has been mentioned previously is that not only is a current state of knowledge and skill a consequence of environmental and infrastructural factors, but induced changes in these learning areas will create environmental and infrastructural pressures. Not only will expectations change, but they will have to be planned for in all sectors – including schools and universities. In this regard the suggestion is that the optimal situation can best be attained by the closest possible co-operation of all those involved in the field of management education – including perhaps those organisations investing in a particular country.

As a cautionary note the danger of oversophistication of expectations has to be mentioned. Real problems can emerge if a developed talent is left idle. There is probably no greater disincentive than being given a set of skills and being denied the opportunity to put them to work. To be effective the level of sophistication in the planned learning has to be appropriate to the planned application of knowledge.

As a repeated note of reality – be it again uncomfortable to some countries – it has had to be reinforced that there are situations where localisation, in the form of placing local people in key positions as a declared policy, can be close to catastrophic. Ascendency to key positions in such cases can be taken for granted by the chosen few. There can be total lack of motivation and the desire to either learn or work can be destroyed. Certainly there will be a denial of earned recognition and an unwillingness to expose inadequacies.

Here we must return to structured staff succession. Each emerging country owes it to itself to reinforce the situation of earned promotion. In this regard the 'divine right' approach is no criterion for real self-respect – no criterion for either personal or country advancement.

Here it is essential to acknowledge the work, the effort and the evident pride that is a feature of constructive localisation. Here is real courage and perhaps never better exampled than by a headline 'We'll do Better' appearing in the Papua New Guinea *Post Courier* of 12 August 1977. This headline was the lead into an article written by the Chairman of the Public Service Commission – an article which illustrated perfectly the use of an appropriate level of sophistication. While the content deserves to be quoted in full, selected extracts will serve to illustrate both the honest self-analysis and the objective recognition of the consequences.

> With Departments having developed a clear idea of what has to be done, and in what order, it will be possible to produce a realistic picture of requirements for the particular staff necessary.
>
> This is a major development. Departments so far have largely been concerned with replacement of expatriates. It has been difficult to look ahead and make reliable estimates of the sorts of qualifications which will be required, both for national and overseas staff, over any specified time-span.
>
> One particular advantage will be to identify in advance those areas where specialised forward training is going to be needed, and the numbers the Government will need.
> It will also allow orderly localisation of the remaining sectors – as much as possible – of Government employment.
> Of course localisation started well before Self-government, with a slow, steady and systematic approach.
> Very early on, unskilled positions were localised, followed by the semi-skilled, with a start also made on certain skilled occupations.
>
> However, it is a characteristic of skilled and upper-level managerial positions that not only formal training qualifications are needed, but also practical experience. Before Independence there just was not enough preparation of this category of National staff, which is a major reason for the apparent lag in localisation of many senior-level posts within the Government.
>
> It was seen as vital to place National officers into sensitive policy-making areas as quickly as possible.

These officers were placed in a difficult position – their training had had to be accelerated and compressed. Very great demands were placed upon these officers. Under the circumstances, the program of localisation in this respect, has met the demands and expectations of the Government and people.

The country has expected almost superhuman results from lots of its public servants, considering in how short a span they have been expected to acquire a high degree of managerial and other technical expertise.

The problems we do have are not peculiar to Papua New Guinea. Every new State is well aware of them. They are problems not only of people but also of new technologies.

We know we can do better in the times ahead. We must and we will.

Moreover both the headline and the article were preceded by a summary of Government staff statistics providing a clear and candid picture of the country's public service staffing.

To put what is written here into perspective it needs also to be mentioned that the same newspaper carried stories of severe tribal fighting and mutilation in the more remote areas of the country, of the need for the media to reach the people in the villages, of leadership seminars – and of a seemingly neglected promise to give greater prominence to women in the affairs of the country.

A touch of hard reflection was added to the total picture of localisation in an editorial some few days later.[11]

It is learning on the job the hard way. When we make mistakes they are our own. We don't have people above us to cover up. But even from our mistakes we can learn, and add to the store of experience each of us has to acquire so quickly.

---

11 For a further situational example see also p. 149.

Aiding government relations

Instead of a resistant and grudging attitude to a local bureaucracy, which in fact, except perhaps for a natural combination of uncertainty and the desire to be absolutely certain, is not so different from that in any country, the development of mutual trust must be one effective way to improve relationships and gain co-operation. Certainly an attitude of conceit will only be self-defeating, as will the expectation that the bureaucracy will be any more prepared than in any other country to be at the beck and call of a foreign organisation.

Some of the proven means of building closer and constructive relationships are:

- To remember at all times that the right to dignity extends to the lowest level of bureaucratic clerk. To adopt any other attitude is not only insulting it is also on act of futility.
- To anticipate requirements so that answers or at least the resource data from which to find the answers are readily available. This will only help to avoid the common – and too often correct – accusation of lack of co-operation.
- This approach can be extended one step further by circulating non-restricted data to the government in advance of their expressed needs. This approach may even serve to direct the government efforts by indicating the type of information that they would best be helped by.
- A form of self-help which also helps others is to prepare a slide or transparency library which can be used as source data to prepare presentations for the various government visitors. Such a step makes for sounder public and government relations than, for example, the customary rush through pre-selected parts of a factory.

In terms of joint effort and effectiveness the optimum channel for gaining understanding, co-operation and open relationships is through the training effort:

- The fact of having an in-company programme, even if designed for entirely organisational needs, is in itself an aid – particularly if such programmes demonstrate concern for the problems and interests of the host country – and more particularly if they demonstrate a real intention to train local staff for more responsible positions.

- Invitations to local guest speakers on such programmes is an obvious aid to good relationships not only as a means of demonstrating interest, but also as recognition of promoting a two-sided relationship.

- In some areas this approach can be taken one step further by issuing invitations to selected third party participants to attend specialist course and discussion groups. This is likely to be effective at the middle levels where there is an unembarrassed desire to learn, and where, for example, the customs regulations of a country can be discussed at that level without fear of loss of face or dignity. There is certainly a need for caution to protect the interests of both parties, but, again, nothing is lost by making a controlled effort.

- Scholarships provide a further means of gaining good will, particularly if such scholarships are offered in areas where the country has a need for advanced technical training. Incidentally, these same scholarships can also be the optimum form of recruitment.

- A combination of approaches has also been tried with real success by some organisations in utilising the technical training possibilities within their own organisations as a training ground for the most outstanding of high school or university graduates.

The essential point is that it is responsible to assume that any host country government will appreciate evidence of interest and positive intent with regard to the in-country situation.

Practical guiding principles

To put the foregoing examples and suggested solutions in perspective it is essential to return to the most basic practical issues.

The essential starting point in breathing life into a vision and driving and motivating towards a new reality is indeed to know where you are going and to have a well-structured picture of the future.

As has been mentioned, the tools are planning and a real knowledge of the environment and the required resources. The skills are clear: first, the ability to persuade not only through figures and charts, but through clear and exampled recognition of the realities of mutual interest, through dynamic word pictures of what can be achieved, through exampled confidence and through the courage to place trust in others; second, the ability to show and earn respect by keeping all statements realistic and meaningful in a way that respects the intelligence of others.

The project manager, with his model of the factory-to-be and his handful of locally recruited engineers, can be a vital force of influence. The locally recruited man, if well selected and sent to the United States or Europe for training, can be a powerful salesman for the values of any enterprise. But these, and the many other points that have been mentioned have to be placed in the context of an overall approach.

In practical terms, taking known and proven examples from countries as far apart and as different as Taiwan and Tanzania, the various common steps contained in such an approach have included:

- Providing a clear statement of intention that goes beyond the usual permit and license applications.

  Such a statement requires to be repeated to as many levels of government, banking and business interests as possible. The vehicle for the statement can range through meetings with the highest government officials to the monthly rotary lunch and with such diverse bodies as the local association of engineers to the local authority of housing. The important point is to be selective while of covering all the bases. Great care has to be taken in preparing the statement so that it is always a consistent reflection of the intended reality and not an idle fantasy. Early promises are remembered – not only by bankers, but also by communities who build their own hopes according to their own dreams. If the statement concerns products to be produced examples can be made available. If the statement concerns buildings the project manager's model or at least the plans and landscaped drawings can be at hand. If the statement concerns employment opportunities for qualified staff or staff to be qualified, long-term training and development programmes can be made ready. If it is clear that labour cost is a decisive factor the point can be acknowledged, but the significance of labour content, of shipping and distribution costs, and of all of the other cost factors, can also be described.

- Demonstrating a non-critical understanding for the economic and infrastructural realities.

Such a demonstrated understanding provides the opening to discuss also the contribution that can be made. Mutual interest can best be developed if the self-interest of the various parties is acknowledged in the early stages.

- Recruiting against the background of what will be rather than what is.

The gap can be acknowledged and discussion can indicate how it will be closed. Commencing salaries and wages can demonstrate understanding of local practices without causing immediate embarrassment to local employers, but earning potentials can still be discussed. Growth can be discussed at every opportunity and a feeling of organisation history can be introduced to show evidence of past growth.

- Informing always against the background of the vision.

What happened in the first quarter of 1978 is better projected against the long-term plan than against the last quarter of 1977. Talking in terms of progress against the long-term base will encourage belief in what can be accomplished.

- Including local people in the decision-making.

In some countries it will be true that for the first two years such people will attend decision-making meetings without saying a significant word – but they are observing and learning and the day will come when their confidence will let them speak at a level often not believed possible.

- Delegating successively.
  In many countries the adage 'let them learn by their mistakes' can be a total disaster as the loss of face arising from the mistake can be for ever inhibiting. As always it is a matter of knowing the probable reactions before taking the action.
- Investing in people and at the same time providing reasons for pride.
  A recent example from Korea saw a group of engineers, specially selected using local as well as imported techniques so that all who were selected had an immediate reason for a feeling of success, departing for Europe all wearing jackets with the national emblem of Korea – not of the organisation – clearly stitched on the breast pocket.
- Using local customs.
  If it is customary to have religious or other ground-breaking ceremonies, if new machines are to be blessed – by all means the practice should be followed. All such events symbolise growth in a local situation.
- Entering the community.
  The other alternative is to ignore it.
- Anticipating an equivalent level of intelligence.
  Not to do so is not only an insult, it will also determine organisation behaviour and attitudes.
- Growing with the experience.
  An American remains an American, an Englishman remains an Englishman. All have their own values and ways. But by the whole process of adapting and remaining open-minded it is possible to learn to question old convictions and to become a totally larger person.

The transfer of technology – through people

The six major areas for discussion at the May 1977 Conference on International Economic Cooporation (CIEC) in Paris, were commodities, resource and development aid, international debts, energy, capital investment and trade.

One report described the meeting as being:

> between the world's economic haves and have nots –
> with the industrialised rich offering the under-
> developed poor some aid but mostly promises.

While it is possible to agree or disagree with the content
of the agenda, and while the condescending undertones in
the report could be debated, the reality of the relationship
remains people-based, knowledge-based and technology-
based.

The international transfer of technology is increasingly a
subject of great importance in the interaction between
countries. Understandably it is also a subject of some
passion. Unfortunately sometimes these passions tend to
obscure the critical importance of the people aspects that
are vital to making it effective.

On the one hand there are the grand pronouncements
which usually contain certain elements from the following
generalised formula:

> We have an absolute commitment to continue a
> soundly based dialogue with the developing countries.
> Our target is the achievement of a constructive and
> mutually beneficial economic cooperation. We pledge
> ourselves to support the economic development and
> growth of those poorer countries …

On the other hand with the same degree of generalisation
the statement from those receiving the technology also has
a set pattern:

> We believe that technology, no matter where
> developed, belongs to all countries. The points to be
> settled are that the provision of aid in this area must
> contribute to the general, social and economic goals
> within countries. Fair terms leading to eventual local
> ownership are essential …

Added to this chemistry of relationships are the various
economic communities and associations such as the EEC,

ASEAN, OAU, ECOWAS, to name only a very few. These pockets of regional strength each have their own range of objectives and philosophies. In this context it is perhaps both useful and of interest to provide a quotation from an Organisation of African Unity (OAU) statement dated May 1977:

> they should help us to strengthen our resolve and to define our goals and to realise that there is no final solution to the problems of human nature, that there is still an overriding need for us to understand one another better so as to consolidate the unity and solidarity of our states, and that in the survival of our organisation lies the future, freedom and dignity of Africa.

Putting to one side the political overtones, the remainder of the statement refers to such matters as mineral wealth, agricultural export products and water resources 'which are acknowledged to be the greatest in the world'. Reference is also made to the 'dearth of managerial and middle grade personnel with labour being generally unskilled', and this point is developed as follows:

> the problem ... is also being tackled by stepping up the educational programmes in all countries. Primary and secondary education is now compulsory in some countries, while enrolments for primary, secondary and university places have increased quite considerably in the whole of Africa since independence. Technical education has not been neglected.

The concluding statement however provides added value and invites deeper interest by its note of hard reality:

> African countries realise the limitations imposed by their sparsely distributed population. They are also aware that some industrial ventures could best be promoted successfully only if such ventures serve a group of neighbouring nations with adequate communication links ... The causative problems have

been identified. Political will and climate now exist for rapid industrialisation. However Africa would not be able to take full advantage of these potentials with its present shortage of investment funds, lack of industrial skills, of technical know-how and of qualified personnel. In these areas outside help is needed.

While the quotations presented here are localised they are intended only as being illustrative of the backgrounds and indeed of the realities. Further, they are intended again to reinforce the hard facts of the very practical aspects of people development that have been emphasised earlier.

Clearly the transfer of technology takes place through people and has to be seen as an integrated process with planned adaptation to local situations. Successful implementation will rely on desophistication of process application and the developed knowledge, attitudes and skills of people. Equally clearly there are many other factors such as capital intensiveness, process complexity, technology continuity, labour utilisation, export potential, competition with local industry, contribution to the local economy, as well as the facts of national passion and finance mentioned earlier.

In terms of people development there are also guiding constraints. All of the relevant elements of any one process have to be learned over a related time scale. Bearing in mind that any one process may require many levels and layers of expertise the familiarisation and training process needs to be as clearly defined and sequenced as the process itself. The purpose of the transfer must also be as clear as the process and if, for example, it is related to a specific product or to a method of manufacture, the flow of technology is best accompanied by information regarding every possible detail from the stage of design to that of ultimate use – in a way that is within a given level of understanding. Not withstanding all other aspects, the foundation for success will be the people-development skills of those making the new knowledge available and the meaningful involvement of those who are the recipients and end-users of that knowledge. These must always be the fundamental elements.

Once again to reinforce what has been written earlier, in so far as the transfer of technology implies 'change' the possibility for more effective and rapid implementation will increase when people can be given a feeling of their own vital role in the process of change. Expectations arising from the end results of change can be converted into living motivators so that the possibilities of change in terms of life style or quality of life – at any stage of industrial development – can become focal points in effective technology transfer. When the change process becomes part of motivation, change can be better understood as a challenge.

Conclusion

- The selection of the most suitably qualified staff of appropriate level and potential is the one most fundamental step in the whole process of people development.
- Training those involved in the selection process is therefore one of the main and most critical early priorities.
- The placing of too great an emphasis on those who speak and communicate in English or some other 'convenient' language can be the first step to long-term disaster.
- The purpose of any selection method is as far as possible to place people in situations where they will have a fair chance of being both successful and well-adjusted.
- Being usually a socially acceptable practice, the employment interview is likely to be the most commonly used selection tool.
- The job-description aid to interviewing requires special care so that it does not become in any sense restrictive to guided initiative or performance.
- Talent resources are likely to be limited but to bargain for talents and skills that have been developed by others offers no long-term solution. Only well-informed local knowledge and soundly structured

training and people development can provide the real answer.

- To be totally effective, training and development programmes must be supportive to immediate and longer-term organisational goals. The additional implication in this context is that any organisation philosophy must of necessity include an expressed or implicit attitude and approach to those tasks.

- The essential ingredients of such an approach are that it should reflect needs and resources, a feeling for the dynamics involved, an awareness of the environmental context, and that it should be structured according to a planned approach.

- Being itself a learning process the application of dynamic planning can become part of the total learning process.

- In a situation where the environment itself is tuned to change there remains a fundamental need to build in a feeling for structured approaches and a sense of deliberate direction. The essential element is commitment through involvement.

- Descriptions of ideal situations and solutions are essential for learning but acknowledgment of the troublesome problem areas are equally important if learning is to be converted into reality. The tools for this conversion are training, development, education, exampled behaviour, evidence of structured and environment-related approaches and constructive dialogue with the appropriate local authorities.

- People development in its broadest sense can best be pursued as a joint activity with governments, education authorities and industry in mutually supporting roles. Viewed in such a context people development becomes a key ingredient of resources development and therefore deserves the same degree of planning as any other economic resource.

- Recognition of this in-context fact-regarding people development can only assist in the achievement of National Development Plans and in making the transfer of technology more effective. Change and the emerging challenge can become motivating.

5 The expatriate question

The need for a deliberate process

As was mentioned briefly in Chapter 1, strategy derives from the environment and, at the earliest possible stage, the fundamental research into the environment will include such questions on such matters as:

- the existing and required people skills
- the trends of social and cultural change
- the speed of such trends
- an analysis of likely attitudes to the developments that have been considered for implementation, and in the case of an investing company an analysis of the normal characteristic methods and philosophies of the company
- an analysis of the various factors that are normally considered motivating within that environment
- a resultant analysis of the leadership styles that have proven, or are likely to prove, appropriate.

While these are only examples of a host of questions and, while the question content will vary in emphasis between environments, the last three are clearly relevant to the successful employment and utilisation of expatriates. The implication of the questions is that:

- governments seeking the assistance of foreign staff and companies entering new environments are aware that their intended developments must take into account the feelings and attitudes of the people within the environment.
- the implied pre-calculation regarding motivation ensures that there is a prior effort to understand the most appropriate approaches to the problems of change.

– particular attention is given to the total question of management style. Here the solution is concerned not only with the style expectation that is dominant but also with the selection of expatriates who have the capacity for flexibility of style.

The overriding implication is of course that the selection of expatriates should be a deliberate process that takes full account of the local circumstances. The accompanying underlying thought is that discussion of the subject in such deliberate terms serves to overcome those emotional objections which centre on the rather *ad hoc* appointment of expatriate staff.

The facts behind the emotions

Certainly, it is absolutely reasonable for a country to wish to have its own people in positions of responsibility. What then are the non-emotional reasons for a government or a company to sanction the employment of expatriate staff?

- The transfer of technology requires that people with a commanding knowledge of the technology be involved in its application. Essentially this is a question of simple efficiency. It involves both expert know-how and the ability to train others. It is a matter of return or investment for all parties and, in some cases, can be rather long-term so that the application of knowledge can be tested over time.
- Creating a new reality out of a vision can require the closing of a knowledge gap. Such a gap can encompass the total span of management activities so that inputs are required in every sector. This is in fact the normal and natural situation that arises from the investigation of existing and required skills. Whether, in this case, it is short- or long-term depends as much on the ability to learn as on the ability to transfer learning.
- The sheer size of the investment by an organisation operating 'overseas' requires that it safeguard its own interests. This involves an enormous effort on the part of the organisation to understand, to enter into and

integrate with the financial and people aspects of a country. Such an investment can never be short-term and the fact of entry into an environment could reasonably be expected to imply the desire to remain in and to become part of the environment.

- In the case of the international companies that operate in many diverse environments the ingredient that is essential to ultimate success is the quality of the personal relationships both within and between countries. The building up of such relationships is dependent on interchange and understanding that is to the mutual advantage of all who are involved. Success in this aspect can only come as a result of a deliberate policy which includes the development of the so-called third country nationals and the development of an expatriate group that itself has a broader cultural base than that of the country of the investing company.

Several other basic points could be mentioned but the probability is that they could be categorised within the four reasons given above. Essentially it is a matter of pragmatism and there is indeed little room for emotion in the early stages. Problems however can and do occur in the later stages of development and it is here that real maturity is required both by companies and by host governments.

To phase out expatriates simply because of national pride is itself not a sufficient reason, but then for a company to retain expatriates in the face of sufficiently trained local staff is to invite the antagonism that plagues this extremely important aspect of the process of people development.

Another important factual aspect is to give proper consideration to the reasons why a minority of people from the so-called developed countries are prepared to live abroad – particularly at a time when the comfort expectations of the great majority appear to be of such paramount importance.

Here the first point is indeed that there is no place 'abroad' for the comfort-seekers. What then are the reasons why families elect to live and work in environments other than their own?

- For the pragmatist there is the incentive of additional

salary, a level of life style that, while it tends to be artificial, is sometimes higher than in the home country. There is the element of an inflated or 'command' position and responsibility and, of course, there is the career value of another experience.

- For the romantic there is the excitement of life in another culture, the chance to expand horizons and to put one's inherent values to the test.
- For the practical man there is above all the opportunity to be exposed to individual responsibility and to discover the satisfaction that can come from working with and through another cultural pattern.

All of these can be incorporated in the reality of the answer and all are well understood by the people in the emerging countries. But there are many more factors that emerge as being of equal or greater significance:

- It is a matter of working in a world of limited facts. Understanding requires the ability to 'feel' a situation and action requires the courage to react and interact on the basis of those feelings.
- Being exposed as an 'example' can imply a constraint on behaviour as the example has sometimes to be set in terms of the norms of another set of expectations.
- A different culture usually has the added consequence of a different language, different food, different customs, a different climate and a new set of social patterns. For the adventurous these are only added ingredients to the adventure. For the unadventurous or the timid they can be the cause of both physical and mental indigestion and, in creating simple unhappiness, can be reasons for increasing and mutual dissatisfaction and resentment.
- Family unity has its greatest test when it is removed from the supportive backdrop of a familiar environment. The props that exist amongst family and friends can only be fully appreciated by their absence. The husband-and-wife relationship is at best returned to the pre-television era. At worst, when the reaction to new experiences cannot be shared through similar or discussable reactions, the emerging differences can only be destructive.

- While the greatest satisfaction can be the self-knowledge that comes with the mirrored realities of being totally exposed, this is only true if the image resembles the expectations. The potential gain or loss of self-confidence, the consequences in terms of effectiveness and, the ultimate long-term career effects will be directly related to this revelation.

Understanding of these facts of expatriate life can be critical to the effectiveness of the role of the expatriate in the whole process of people development. It is fundamental that they be understood by all those involved in the process of their appointment. Taken together they account for the care and attention given to expatriate contracts, to the sending out programmes and to the problems related to re-entry.

When discussed in unemotional terms and in those cases where there is an on-going dialogue with the local authorities, when seen alongside the manpower planning and replacement schedules, and when placed within the context of the deliberate and structured training and development of local people, the whole problem of localisation immediately has a sound base. The essence of the solution to the emotive issues is centred on the word 'dialogue'.

'There'

Clearly it is possible to avoid the situation where the brightest, or most aggressive, or the best salesman, or the longest-serving manager from the New York, London or Tokyo office is sent out 'to take care of our interests there'.

Whereas 'there' was once imagined to be some universal distant place other than 'here', it is now recognised as being unique. The essential skill is to obtain a prior understanding of a specific 'there'.

This unique 'there' is a country. It is the society mentioned in the Introduction. It is the subject of the research mentioned in Chapter 1. It is a specific environment. It is a situation in a particular stage of development. It is people with certain values and patterns of behaviour. It is a set of circumstances that result from the forces of history and time. It is above all else in this context a pattern of human demands.

It is never easy to design a specification of the man most likely to succeed 'there'. Neither is there an endless supply of managers, technologists and specialists who can face each country's unique set of challenges. Nevertheless it is possible to isolate criteria for the selection of the most appropriate men from those that are available.

Consequences for expatriate selection

Clearly in all cases involving the appointment of expatriate staff – whether at the invitation of a government, by the initiative of an international organisation, or in the initial or later stages of the growth of an investing company – their selection and their own subsequent development will be fundamental to the success or failure of the whole concept of people development.[1]

As has been said there is no magic formula but there are certain personal elements that can be identified. The priority order of the following factors will depend to quite an extent on the intended location and, while it is certain that no one man can completely satisfy all the requirements, the mere fact of having a checklist will be an aid to those making the selection. Clearly, also, knowledge of the readily apparent effort behind the selection should be a source of reassurance to those countries receiving the benefit of the advice and assistance of experts in their fields.

In listing the points that follow, the assumption is made that the ability to perform exists – that is, the capacity to exercise a particular skill, or professionalism, or the technical knowledge to carry out a particular function. Such a list of factors can never hope to be complete but neither can this be a reason to hesitate to try to formulate at least some of the most critical:

- *The desire to work within and with another culture.*

    Without this most basic ingredient the best managers

1 For an earlier guiding reference see p. 42.

and most qualified specialists will be unlikely to achieve long-term success.

The man who has to be 'sold' the idea of spending or, for career reasons, 'investing' a few years as an expatriate is the least likely to succeed. If he is oversold he can only become disappointed, and if his only motivation is the growth of his career his personal ambition is likely to reflect itself in lack of long-term interest and lack of patience. Such a man will be seeking spectacular short-term results and all too often these can only be achieved to the detriment of the longer-term interests.

It must also be said though that the desire to work in another culture is in itself insufficient unless many of the other capacities are also present.

● *Genuine interest in helping others to develop.*

Just as the man who wants the headlines will seldom give credit to others, the technician who lives only for his speciality may well neglect the knowledge requirements of others. While not all expatriates can be trained discussion leaders or teachers, those that want to can readily acquire the basic skills of helping others to learn. Certainly the man without experience in this field will require guidance and ideally will be thoroughly trained as part of his preparation.

Any unresolved shortcomings in regard to this criterion can serve to defeat the whole longer-term purpose of expatriate selection.

● *Awareness of own environment.*

The man who is aware of the various forces at work within his own familiar environment will probably display a similar interest in other environments. This implies the capacity not only to enquire but also the natural restraint to know when to remain non-critical. The additional associated ingredient is the broadness of mind not only to be interested, but also to demonstrate interest.

Such a man will readily find satisfactions and will quickly develop an awareness of his surroundings that will enable him to become both respected and effective.

- *Self-respect/self-knowledge.*

  Self-respect that is supported by realistic values and derives from self-knowledge will provide an awareness of the environmental influences and will promote recognition of the needs of others for self-respect and for dignity.

  Clearly the man who possesses this characteristic will not only have the capacity to resist both the mental and the moral temptations, but he is also likely to possess the inner strength to be able to win the respect of others.

- *Self-control/self-knowledge.*

  Awareness of the importance of his own exampled behaviour and attitudes is fundamental to success. This implies an additional dimension of self-knowledge regarding a personal style of managing and an awareness that no one style will be appropriate either to all circumstances or to all people. While this aspect of style flexibility is inherent to some, in other cases it will have to be learned deliberately.

  Such knowledge provides an essential key to the ability to counsel, to encourage, to discipline, to motivate and to instruct. In addition, in this context, it can be a vitally important factor in terms of self-control when faced with new and stressful situations.

- *Flexible approach to own speciality.*

  The expatriate will only earn lasting respect for what he is and for what he does and, in terms of his own speciality, he must have sufficient knowledge to allow him to think flexibly within it. The more specific his speciality the more difficult this will be.

  In this regard there is a relationship with the ability to desophisticate knowledge and with the ability to make new knowledge meaningful. The task in terms of the selection process is to predict this capacity in the knowledge-centred specialist. Without such a man the transfer of knowledge cannot be attempted but without such a capacity it can never succeed.

- *Business interest beyond own speciality.*

  Enthusiasm for a point of detail has to be extendable to enthusiasm for the whole. Any developing activity tends to be results-related and as projects progress, increased market share and turnover become the daily conversational diet.

The injection of enthusiasm over a long period also requires that this breadth of interest can be both demonstrated and communicated so that it can be shared with others.

- *Intuitive 'company' feeling.*

In another context 'loyalty' could perhaps be a substitute term, but in this case something more is intended. Here the purpose is to develop in others an intuitive company-or institution-oriented reaction to any problem. Clearly this is impossible if the expatriate is not always able to example this reaction.

The potential for confusion which can arise from the uncontrolled criticism by an expatriate of the activities of his 'home office' will be clear. The home office visitor who fails to recognise the need for a local loyalty can of course be equally damaging.

Added to these situations is the fact of existing and undeniable country loyalties and, in many cases, the loyalties of local staff to previous employers.

- *Mental adaptability and mobility.*

A less apparent criterion arises from the fact that constant switches of attention will be tiring for those used to long periods of concentration. For this reason an effort must be made to predict reactions, as such a requirement is inevitable even for the solo specialist.

- *Problem-solving capability and innovating Skill.*

In a climate of change and development the problems of planning, establishing priorities, task setting and delegating, all contain a greater element of uncertainty. They all require a preparedness to take risks and to try new approaches utilising limited resources. The variables to be considered will cover a wider range and will require a revised and changing set of weightings.

The need for solutions will be more immediate and, regardless of the level of the decision-maker, will be more personally demanding.

- *Sense of achievement and resilience.*

  The desire to achieve is an evident necessity but this has to be predicted alongside the accompanying ability to maintain that desire against all levels of frustration – not necessarily with people, but more with underdeveloped infrastructures and with large numbers of sometimes very small problems.

  Here it has to be appreciated that in most cases the expatriate expert no longer has the small army of only slightly lesser experts to buffer him and to take care of the pin-pricking details. These are the people that he has to develop and, unless he does so, such problems are likely to remain as a lasting and increasing factor in his daily frustrations.

- *Visionary quality.*

  This skill of drawing a word picture of what can be is essential in relating the learning process to the total process of change. It is difficult to predict but, essentially, it requires the ability to see both a current and a potential total picture, the skill to relate widely assorted and rapidly changing variables, and the courage and faith to trust others.

  It is a matter of the capacity to breathe life into an idea, to plant it firmly in the minds of others, and to create belief that it can become a reality.

- *Developed social skills.*

  Community life itself can be a new experience for many. Added to this, and complicating the predictability, is the fact that, while in the home country the expatriate would be a highly unlikely host to high government officials, such an event could be a regular requirement in the host country.

- *Capacity to be a non-standard man.*

  The standard man with the standard approaches to the standard problems is best kept in a standard situation. The textbook mentality that relies on the tested formulas is more likely to aggravate than to succeed. The standard teachings are of course essential mental disciplines but the reality is that very often the old and familiar problems require new and unfamiliar solutions. Certainly each new problem requires a more open-ended and courageous mental approach.

Here the predictors of success are not less difficult than in the other cases but the man who is more oriented to focus on solutions is more likely to succeed than the man who is problem-oriented. The problem-analysis and decision-making process tend to become compressed in time and the expert in the techniques will not always have time to find all the familiar inputs. In this regard the expatriate has to learn for himself the art of desophisticating his own knowledge.

- *A wife with similar capacities.*

The most fortunate, and perhaps also the most effective, expatriate is the man who can share his growth experience with his wife. Certainly the least happy expatriate is the man who cannot.

While the once popular interviewing of wives seems to have become less acceptable, as long as it is not practiced there will always remain room for uncertainty. The contradictory feature here is that with the generally increasing role of women in the emerging as well as the developed countries, the choice of expatriate wives has never been a more important issue.

These then are some of the criteria that can best be seen as being complimentary to the usual in-company or institutional list of traits and characteristics. The suggestion is that they could prove useful to both the expatriate selection process and to the process of preparing selected expatriates.

Underlying all of them is the ability to communicate which in this sense means more than learning a foreign language. Here it implies the willingness to understand, to listen, to exercise patience, to repeat, to instruct, to avoid assumptions, to recognise that adaptation is indeed multidirectional and mutual, to make an effort to make new knowledge meaningful and to demonstrate vocal and visual respect for a local situation.

A list of negative aspects of equal length could also be provided but a few examples may be sufficient to make the point. Cliché-type labelling is a ready temptation. The expressions 'we tried to help them but they are basically lazy' or 'sure, they are good at a conference, but watch them in action', only serve to create a we/they situation which will create a spiral of mutual ill will. Another negative comes from the expatriate who is always ready to complain about his housing, his servants, the climate or his salary. It is true that a sense of responsibility in another society can no more be taken for granted that it can in our town, but it has no chance of taking root when the examples provided are irresponsible. Such a sense can best be developed through example and such example may necessarily have to be a conscious effort. It is reasonable that local people will generally tolerate each other's below-standard performance, at least in the learning period, but they will not easily tolerate poor performance or effort from a foreign manager, particularly if he has the habit of reacting against the local conventions and customs. Further, foreign managers who live always within their own national community will be as likely to appeal to the local people as those who try to adapt to the local culture in its entirety. There is nothing quite so pathetic as the man who attempts to enact a culture without really understanding it.

The simple fact is that there are certain, almost invariable, stages in an expatriate's period in any one country – but particularly in an emerging country. First, there is the initial anticipation tinged with a touch of apprehension. Then come the agonies of arrival with the housing, schooling and initial task frustrations. This is rather quickly followed, almost by way of compensation, by the 'expert in local and country affairs' stage, which lasts until the expatriate knows enough to realise how little he knows. With this knowledge comes the really effective working period that also brings with it the real depth of understanding and the love of both country and people. All too soon after this comes the realisation that the task is done and the feeling of not really wanting to move on.

Seen through the eyes of a senior local manager, 'It's just like a new pair of shoes. Just as they are finally feeling comfortable it's time for them to be replaced.'

Understanding through empathy

There is no doubt that both for foreign managers and for the local people in senior positions their management attitudes must always be on display. Their competence is tested at every step. The problem is usually looked at from the perspective of the foreign manager and it is a relatively easy matter to dramatise his role.

Perhaps though there is also something to be gained by trying to see the situation from the point of view of the local people who are being developed. A man in this situation is asked to make an almost total reassessment of his values. Time and again he is faced not only with new problems, but also with new answers to old problems. While being educated he is constantly, even if indirectly, asked to educate those who are developing him. In many cases he is asked to exercise a discipline which he is only starting to comprehend himself. He is expected to be both a catelyst between cultures and to maintain his place in both. His abilities are being stretched in all directions. His behaviour, manners and attitude to work itself are undergoing changes he could never have imagined, and, he is expected to exercise his education and use his initiative to a degree and with a speed that makes each new decision or recommendation a unique experience. Furthermore, he knows that he will be judged on the basis of criteria that are far removed from the previous central issues of his life.

These are vital considerations, for the essential ingredient that must go hand-in-hand with the desire to understand, the ability to desophisticate, the skill to make learning meaningul, strength to refrain from the easy temptation to resort to popular labels and the wit to enjoy the experience, is the ability to emphathise and to be ready to see the experience from another man's point of view. To succeed in doing this through language and across cultures depends mainly on the depth of the first requirement – the desire to understand.[2]

2 Some more light-hearted advice is provided in Appendix XI, p. 232

Conclusion

- The selection of expatriate staff must be seen as a deliberate and balanced process that takes full account of the local environmental, infrastructure and people circumstances.
- The main reasons for engaging expatriate staff include effective transfer of technology, the closing of a knowledge gap, the protection of a major investment and the building up of people relationships on the broadest possible base.
- Avoidance of the potential problems arising from 'isation' calls for intelligent and non-emotive reasoning from both the host country and the home country and for continuing dialogue regarding manpower planning and replacement schedules.
- The selection process can only be of benefit if a prior effort is made to derive a set of criteria that extend beyond the ability to perform.
- Expatriate success will depend as much as anything else on the ability to communicate, to relate and to interact with empathetic understanding.

6   Key points and summarised conclusions

Summarised conclusions and further inferences

To summarise, it is possible to draw a number of conclusions and inferences that have general validity. While many of these are specifically directed towards the emerging country aspect, there are others that have a more universal relevance.

- In order to be effective in terms of action any comparative consideration of the developed and longer-industrialised countries and the emerging countries must be faced honestly and objectively. Pretence can only lead to ambiguous action. Denial of the differences, can only serve to diminish the essential differences in the application of the learning methods and to make impossible the transition of environment-related knowledge.
- The quality of change depends to a large extent on the management of its introduction and, as the real essence of change comes from within, the development of managers is fundamental. Change itself is, however, concerned with society, and a society is – people.
- People and the environment in which they live are the reality. Development, being concerned with change, is concerned with a new reality. People development is therefore an environment-and accomplishment-related investment in bringing about that new reality.
- In such a climate the new knowledge that is valued is that which can be seen to be appropriate. Effective investment then becomes a matter of the selective application of concepts and practices. The inference

then is that where any form of results-oriented cultural inferface is involved the process of change also involves a willingness for multidirectional and mutual interchange and adaptation.

• Just as it is unlikely that the structure of a society and the value systems of people will always be totally unique it is also unlikely that the problems they encounter when facing the consequences of change will be totally unique. That there will be shade of difference is inevitable. Recognition of those shades of difference between societies and between countries is as vitally important as acknowledging the similarities. It is in fact these two things taken together that can make the application of new knowledge sufficiently flexible to be meaningful to all societies and to all countries. The concept of the common denominators between countries does not in itself deny these differences. It does provide a basis for comparison, it does provide a basis for the search for resources, but the reality remains that the most fundamental issue is the application of knowledge.

• Before a future reality can be believable it has first to be seen as being achievable. This requires that new knowledge be communicated in terms not only of new learning, but also in terms of new understanding. The non-essential sophistications can become barriers and learning that are practical in terms of the environment and stated in terms of accomplishments to be achieved is likely to be the most effective. This implies a relationship with expected results and provides a sense of direction to the total process. When such a learning approach is formalised into structured programmes it is likely to succeed best when it can be seen to be meaningful for the future, in context in terms of appropriateness, and motivating in terms of growth. The integration of mutual interest can be given a new dimension by adding to it the concept of vision. By giving people a vision of a new reality and their place in that reality, the whole change process and the inevitability of change itself can be made more readily acceptible.

- Against such a background, theories and concepts can be brought to life and made both dynamic and meaningful. Here the advantage is clearly with the emerging countries as they have a wide fund of knowledge to draw from. In both selecting and utilising resource materials, one of the key points is to ensure that learning is structured in such a way that the basic input patterns can be developed within the context of a particular country.

- Sound implementation will depend for a large part on sound planning, providing always that the planning is in accordance with the practical environmental realities. When structure is added to the longer-term intentions, people development can be seen as an integrated element of business development, industrial development, and, eventually, national development. While execution of the planning needs to be flexible enough to allow for initiatives, it also needs to be sufficiently insistent to provide for on-going learning. Ideally the input of information should flow at a controlled and increasing rate so that learning is progressive and proceeds through the stage of understanding the process of change to the stage of learning how to influence change in terms of goal-setting and resource utilisation.

- The most effective communication of knowledge will occur when the concepts can be clarified and tested against an environmental setting. The frame of reference for the inputs can be relatively firm but the living examples that complete the picture give the concepts their vital lasting impact. When the opportunity is also taken to inject specific and deliberate words and ideas, an organisation language can be created which in turn can be the first step in creating a predetermined organisation culture.

- When structuring programmes it is important to ensure that there are ample opportunities to convert knowledge into action. This applies particularly to the senior staff, who need to test their understanding by putting their knowledge to work. Perhaps the surest way to motivate this group is to pay them the compliment of asking them for opinions – bearing in mind that such a step is indeed only motivating when they can see their opinions leading to action.

- The essential prerequisite for successful people development is the selection of an appropriate number of staff with sufficient potential to enable the planned growth to become a reality. Training the 'selectors', like training the 'trainers', is therefore a priority requirement and for reasons of both convenience and probable social acceptance the employment interview – with supporting and supplementary tests – is likely to prove the most practical method of assessment. Because of the clear need for knowledge of the local language and culture the judgement aspect has at least to be shared with locally trained interviewers. Such a sharing of responsibility does not in any way limit the organisation's responsibility to recruit a balanced labour force. Balance in this case infers that the selection process can be the source of both stability and mobility within the organisation.

- Just as selection needs to be geared to both the constants and the projected changes, training and development programmes can only be truly effective when they are in tune with organisational goals. Both of these activities take place in a particular context and both have to be part of, and contributors to, a total practical organisational philosophy. Such a philosophy must also embrace all of those other factors which, taken together, represent the organisation's approach both to its people and to the host country.

- The process of dynamic planning is the factor that provides the relationship between organisation philosophy and organisation reality. In a situation of high growth, restricted infrastructures, numerous uncertainties, and countless unknowns, planning has to be seen both as a tool of management and as a part of the total learning and change process. Involvement and interaction are the vital ingredients of such a process where the principle purpose is to derive a living picture of what is and what can be. When this is done well both the needs and resources can be highlighted against time and in priority order. These aspects of involvement and interaction can also be used to extend familiarity with management language into the sphere of familiarity with management objectives.

- One of the principal aids to building a spirit of involvement into the dynamics of the business is the discussion of job responsibility areas. Use of this or similar approaches introduces both structured discussion and counselling as an accepted part of the total on-going interaction between people and, where appropriate, between cultures.
- Growth carries with it the pains of growth. These growing pains are not resolved through non-curative criticism, and exampled behaviour ranks alongside training, development and education as the essential means of exposing the capacity for initiative and the potential for development.
- While the process of such exposure can be regarded as an organisational responsibility the process of providing solutions can only be optimised when people development is seen as a joint activity involving all interested parties. Ideally these are likely to be represented by industry, government and local education authorities – each with its own mutually supporting role. Again, the key ingredients are involvement, interaction, on-going dialogue and planning.

   In terms of country development, people development becomes fundamental to economic development and, while the process is enlarged in magnitude, the dynamics of change remain essentially the same.
- The development of people – the enlargement of their expectations within the terms of their own environment – can convert change into challenge and a vision into a reality.
- In those cases where foreign staff are found to be essential elements within the change process, the

further ingredient of empathetic understanding has to
be mentioned as one of the contributors to
constructive achievement through the development
of people.

Brief advice to the multinationals

Those companies who are operating in more than one
emerging country – or for that matter in more than one
country at whatever level of development – will know the
difficulties they face in each one. They will know that in
whatever form the problems present themselves they tend
always in the last resort to reduce themselves to being
people problems. From their accumulation of experience
they will also know that the problems in one country tend
to be similar to the problems in another.

The interesting phenomenon is that, through this
recognition of problem similarity, one of the most
interesting facts of international economic life has emerged.
That is, the link between the identification of common
problem areas with the opportunity for using common
resources. Within the various economic communities this
fact has been longer recognised and it has in those cases
been a linking that emerged through the recognition of
common opportunities. As has been mentioned earlier the
EEC, OAU and ASEAN are only a few examples of those
who are acquiring added strength through association.

Within the content of the previous pages the contributing
factors have been sufficiently exposed and discussed, but to
draw these thoughts together it is possible to restate them as
in Figure 6.1.

The immediate inferences here are that
- utilisation of common resources such as systems
  procedures, methods and even broad policies,
  imposes no inherent threat to the 'unique'
  application aspects within countries;
- in-country effort can be directed towards the
  application aspects so that time, effort and money are
  saved by avoiding international duplication.

The key point in achieving this situation is the

Figure 6.1 In-country application

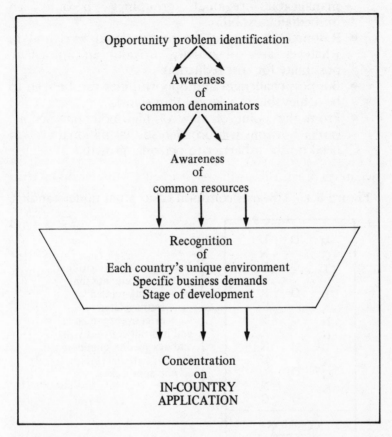

development and the continued repetition of an in-company management language. This language can be the key common denominator across cultures and across the 'traditional' language barriers.

Once this point is recognised the implications expand in both breadth and depth. To illustrate this point, when a number of circles are drawn to represent either the countries or the most promising high potential people in the countries as in Figure 6.2, the range of implications becomes more significant:

- Communication at the international level will gain greater credibility.

- From the point of view of countries, convenient and manageable regional groupings become an immediate possibility.
- Resource sharing at the international level and in whatever area of activity provides an immediate possibility for cost reduction.
- Business challenges and opportunities can be seen to be achievable in a larger framework.
- From the point of view of high-potential people, career horizons will broaden so that national growth need not be a barrier to personal growth.[1]

Figure 6.2　Towards common conceptual understanding

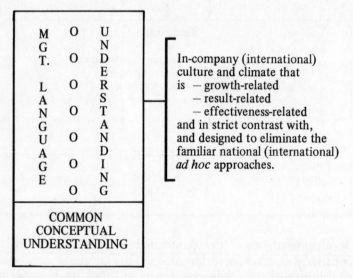

To re-emphasise the point, the success of such an approach will depend on the degree of success achieved in developing the in-company management language, and on the training, coaching and ability of those charged locally with the responsibility for the application of the resources.

---

1 Appendix IV, p. 178, provides an example of some of the problems and opportunities that can arise.

The role of such people is by no means diminished by this approach and these will be people with personal strength and character who will know when to resist a central pressure, when and how to localise it and when to recognise the need for rapid implementation. Such people will have to be developed in the skills mentioned earlier. That is, they will be the experts in local situations who know how to make new knowledge meaningful in a way that respects the intelligence and circumstances of the local situation.

The methods of achieving this goal are for a large part contained within the earlier parts of this book.

Other advice to the multinationals[2] can be very briefly summarised, but the brevity of the comments bears no relation to their critical importance:

- While arrogance is only arrogance and will be simply ignored by some and politely disregarded by others, there are always people who will recognise it for what it usually is – an artificial cover-up of ignorance.
- An engineer in one country feels like an engineer in another country. It isn't enough to˘ make greater claims to better qualifications – it is only important if the difference expresses itself in significantly better performance.
- For those with little experience or exposure, labels come too quickly to the tongue without first being filtered through the mind. 'Corruption' is one of the easiest terms to use and one of the most difficult to define. Local customs and practice should first be understood before they are labelled.
- Complacency, and a superior attitude, are the simplest and most rapid steps to disaster. Equally effective are ridicule and apparent boredom with a local situation.

The comment that comes to mind as the most appropriate local reaction to such forms of behaviour is – 'I know his education is much better – I know his experience is much broader – I know he is here to help me – but I finally lost my patience in trying to help him to help me.'

---

2 Additional specific comment is provided in Appendix X, p. 231.

Local language and culture – the added value

While clearly the advantage will always be with the man who speaks, or makes an effort to speak, the language of the host country, there are also other aspects. Management language and its effect on in-company culture have been mentioned many times – but even this is capable of an element of perhaps unexpected drama.

The case presented here comes from Korea and is used as a concluding example, as a reinforcement of a number of the key concepts – and as an illustration of the fact that the real experts in the culture of a country, and therefore ultimately of the optimum application of the principles of management, are its citizens.

Figures 6.3 – 6.7 form the opening segment of a chart presentation that was designed to encourage and promote the integration of staff-development activities. Certain specific organisation principles have been either removed or generalised but the overall presentation has been used in several other circumstances.

The problem in this case was one of translations, not only of language, but more important, of intention, and the problem manifested itself during the briefing of the very capable senior manager who would be responsible both for the introduction and the follow up. The opening chart, Figure 6.3, proved to be deceptively simple.

Figure 6.3   Increasing effectiveness

```
                                                    1

        An Introduction to the Concept

                    Increasing

                   effectiveness

                     through

                     training

                       and

                   development
```

Figure 6.4 Why training?

2
Why Training?
—to increase effectiveness
—should be seen as a guided investment

The problem (opportunity) emerged with the second chart (Figure 6.4). Suddenly it became necessary to find the words that would correctly convey 'effectiveness' and 'guided investment'. To obtain complete and thorough understanding this required some discussion but what then emerged included and went well beyond the intention.

'*Won dong ryuk*' means, variously, heart power, main course to follow, origin of power, main means, and – with some modification – optimum utilisation – all of which seemed certainly to add up to 'effectiveness'.

'Guided investment' took a little longer, but again the result, '*won tak noi-e sik*' demonstrated the added value. In this case the translation extended into round table decision, decision-making of the whole body and, eventually, to united role in guiding.

The third, fourth and fifth charts (Figures 6.5, 6.6 and 6.7) were first thought to be clear. But they brought the biggest problem and perhaps the most interesting solution, as communication in this case became a matter of leaping

Figure 6.5 What is effectiveness?

3
What is effectiveness?
The extent to which
a man achieves
the output requirements
of his position

across cultures – the essential point being that the man making the presentation had already taken that leap, but in a natural way and over a number of years. Here it was a matter of exposing and attemtping to close the gap in a matter of minutes.

Figure 6.6 What is the measurement?

	4
What is the measurement?	
THE TASK	EXPECTATIONS (RESULTS & TIME)
– (Key tasks) – – – (Other tasks) – – –	

'*Moon-hwa moon myung*' has a particular literal meaning which, when well communicated, extends to the concept of 'philosophic aspiration giving way to practical implication', and can be further stretched to include, 'the science of reality where further guided inspiration can be directed towards the access to new knowledge'.

Figure 6.7 Dynamic task setting

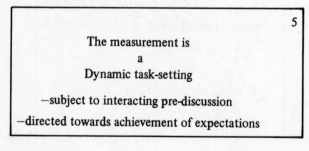

The measurement is
a
Dynamic task-setting

–subject to interacting pre-discussion
–directed towards achievement of expectations

The charts that followed referred, from different points of view, to the concept of the 'development gap' and to the building up of the management language – see Figures 6.8 – 6.12. All of these also received their share of added value in the translation. '*Bun wee*' added a sense of boundary to the concept of breadth, and development was given a sense of growth, time and size, by '*Bal-chun kai-bal*'.

Figure 6.8   Needs analysis

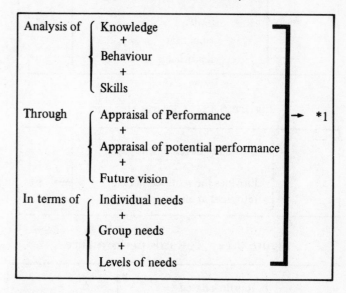

Figure 6.9   Towards planning – exposing the gap

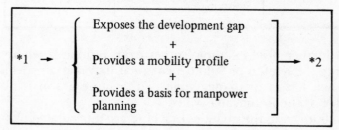

Management language in this case was used in a positive way and the reports were that the discussion sessions provided all the reinforcement that could be desired. The searching for words, the eventual consensus, the subsequent reporting of the English words with their agreed host-country counterparts, were clearly stamped on the living organisation.[3]

Figure 6.10 Towards training

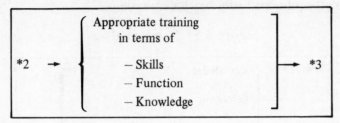

Figure 6.11 Closing the gap

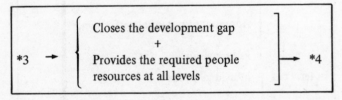

Figure 6.12 Towards performance

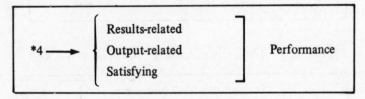

A further brief example comes from Indonesia where a visit to the Kraton or Sultan's Palace at Jogyakarta provides its own lesson in management – the same lesson is also visible at the Ramayana ballet.

In both cases the qualities of a king are represented by six gold symbols: a cock, a lamp, a swan, a dragon, a peacock

---

3 Another detailed example is provided in Appendix VIII, p. 215.

and a deer. These symbols were significant both in the process of selecting a sultan from the ruling family and as a reminder to the sultan of the qualities he must express in his attitudes and actions. Again there is an added value, as the idea of the solid gold symbols represents a continuing philosophy and a breath of dramatic history.

Leadership as it is portrayed in these symbols includes the following:

from the cock   – braveness and virility
from the lamp   – light, an appreciation of the sciences
                    and intelligence
from the swan   – wisdom
from the dragon – power and persistence
from the peacock– pride and prosperity
from the deer   – endurance, activity and the capacity to
                    organise.

As a matter of fact, the present sultan, Hameng Ku Buwomo IX, is also the vice-president of this rapidly emerging country.

Another illustration comes from the Philippines. In this case the approach is both deliberate and very well organised. The Philippines Clearing House, a non-profit-making education service in Manila, offers managers a choice from more than 200 case studies that have for the most part been developed within the Philippines. These cases provide excellent reflections of the cultures and values represented in the various regions within the country in a thoroughly objective manner. While their main purpose is to help local managers to educate their supervisors in the mix of sociological patterns, the cases also have the advantage of providing foreign managers with an understanding of the complexity of relationships and of the facts of management life in the Philippines.

The philosophy at work

As a final concluding example which draws entirely on living reality and reflects the attitude of one multinational, the following quotation is from the closing remarks of a week-long seminar in Nairobi which was attended by some twenty outstanding people from five African countries:

'Together we have learned a great deal ... In this two-way street of learning the initiative has been from the Company – from N.V. Philips's Gloeilampenfabrieken – and from your country managements who provided you with the opportunity.

The essential inputs have been provided and you have perhaps come to see yourselves in the context of this new knowledge.

Self-recognition and self-evaluation is never easy and it takes time to reflect.

The concepts, ideas and philosophies have been exposed in a way that is intended to stretch and extend your abilities. In order to get the full value you are expected to develop these concepts, ideas and philosophies in the context of your companies and your jobs.

You may not find this such an easy task
• others may resist your new ideas and concepts
• change is never easy for the mass of people who rely on the *status quo* for their current status and mainly for their peace of mind.
• it is often easy to give up in the face of such resistance and to be for ever disappointed.

But if you have the urge to achieve you will overcome such resistance and that will perhaps be your first application of the learning experience.

An effort has been made to whet your appetite so that you will want to learn more. It is this area that you will discover yourselves. The desire to achieve, recognition of the importance of self-development, plus, the energy to do something about it – there are the three basic ingredients. A fourth is also important – that is, to discover your own individual level of self-sacrifice. Just how much effort are you really prepared to put into your own development – or will you find excuses not to make the effort?

Remember, your level of success very often depends on your own personally chosen level of self-sacrifice.

Three further points deliberately left until this moment:

First: Passing on this knowledge to others is clearly one of your responsibilities and in the course of this seminar you have acquired some of the relevant skills. Remember that the development of people at any level is an accomplishment-oriented investment in the future. It has to be in line with the goals of the company and to a large extent has to be in tune with the aspiration level of the people.

The essential skill in this regard is counselling and in very many cases the investment in people development is not fully compensated, not because of the quality of the training, but because of the lack of follow up counselling.

Remember to train, teach, and communicate within a level of understanding – always trying to increase that level of understanding. Often there is also the question of adapting the new knowledge; therefore it is a question not only of self-knowledge and knowledge of others, but also knowledge of the demands and requirements of your own environments.

Second: The next point has been referred to but not in detail – that is empathy – the ability to empathise – the skill that can give you real insight into how to motivate, how to communicate, how to lead, how to influence, how to handle problems of change – how to manage.

Empathy is the process of grasping or understanding the other person's point of view – putting yourself in his shoes or viewing a situation or idea through his 'filter'. It can be one of the most valuable, powerful characteristics you can develop to strengthen interpersonal relations, communications and the ability to get things done through and with people.

Third: We touched on integration of interests but did not mention integration of vision – this is in fact the secret of real joint success.

To have a joint goal and to pursue it together can be one of the most exciting, most challenging opportunities in your lifetime. This can be a vision of what a company can become or, what a country can become. One of the most exciting things in life is to have that vision and persuade others to share it.

As said earlier, this whole process of learning is a two-way street. The door to opportunity is open to anybody with a large enough key – the key is self-knowledge – a self-image that allows you to see yourself accomplishing your goals – a realisation that true self-respect comes only from real self-fulfilment. Other people can only provide us with the tools to forge that key. Only you can design and craft it.

Appendices

I   'Understanding' to overcome isolation
II   Strategic planning
III   The staff development and training committee approach
IV   Cross-cultural group dynamics – Fragility, sincerity and self-control
V   The mirror-centred approach; The manager as a professional; Cases for colleagues
VI   Employee counselling – A training aid
VII   The organisation profile approach and the self-declaration form
VIII More language dimensions
IX   Multi-country seminar scenario example
X   Caution regarding short-term expatriate assignments
XI   The Ten Commandments for travellers
XII   Who is judging whom?

Appendix I   'Understanding' to overcome isolation

To emphasise the difficulty of being 'foreign' an example can be taken from one of the world's most industrially developed countries – Japan.

Few nations contain as much self-knowledge, and few nations can be more difficult for the new foreigner who, try as he might, will find it extraordinarily difficult to integrate with his local peer group. These two points are directly related through the fact that once the foreigner has an understanding of the 'self-knowledge' he will, at the same time, come to understand, and even appreciate, the difficulties of integration. The point to emerge is that isolation within an environment can become more tolerable if the reasons for the isolation are understood. At the same time such an understanding can never be a reason to stop or to discourage the effort to integrate – rather, understanding of the reasons and of the various cultural forces must be seen as a means of adding direction and purpose to those efforts.

In his book *The Japanese Businessman*,[1] Mr Masaaki Imai, himself an international Japanese and the emerging expert in this field of internationalisation in Japan, described the self-knowledge aspect as follows:

> There appear to be deeprooted sociological factors that cause the Japanese not to let foreigners into their group at home, while they separate themselves from the local community abroad.

---

1 *The Japanese Businessman* by Masaaki Imai and Paul Norbury is published by Associated Business Programmes (London 1975) and is essential pre-reading for those intending to do business in Japan or for those who find themselves in competition with Japanese business.

Mr Imai goes on to quote Miss Chie Nakane, Professor of social anthropology at Tokyo University who wrote that a Japanese sees his country as:

Ego, with his family located at the centre which is encircled by men of the first category with a second category forming an outer circle. For a corporate executive, his first category would be his colleagues and fellow workers in the same company. His second category would represent all other employees and management of his company, his friends, fellow university graduates, and people whom he has come to know through business or social contact. Beyond this circle, there is an indefinite and undefinable world outside of which he does not even feel it appropriate to apply a particular code of etiquette. He is reluctant to communicate with this world and within himself he recognises, a certain innate hostility towards it.

As Mr Imai points out, it is an unfortunate fact that most foreigners living in Japan belong to the third category.

Nevertheless the foreigner in Japan, or in any other country, must continue to strive for a degree of penetration and, at the same time, must continue his efforts to have his own values understood and respected. Evidently the mental traffic in all such cases flows best when it flows in two directions but, the initial effort is the clear responsibility of the 'guest' in the 'host' country.

Appendix II   Strategic planning

Strategic planning was acknowledged in Chapter 1 as being of vital importance to the whole initiating and investigative stage. Indeed the disciplines contained within this subject and their application within the on-going growth stages of the emerging countries could themselves be the subject of a separate study.

Certainly an outline appreciation is a minimum requirement, and to serve this purpose a copy of a checklist is provided with acknowledgment and thanks to its originator, Mr Ravinder S. Dhingra, who prepared the presentation as part of an article series for *Management*, published by Modern Productions Limited. (See Table A.1.)

Table A 1   Checklist for strategic planning

A. Key legal parameters

  a Differences in legal system and commercial law.
  b Anti-trust laws and rules of competition.
  c Consumer protection laws.
  d Arbitration clauses and their enforcement.
  e Protection of patents, trademarks, brand names and other industrial property rights.
  f Legal restrictions on foreign investment.
  g Flexibility and ease of incorporation.

B. Key political parameters

  a Type of political system; political philosophy, national ideology.
  b Major political parties, their philosophy, and their policies.

   c Stability of the government
- Changes in political parties
- Changes in government

   d Assessment of nationalism and its possible impact on political environment and legislation.

   e Assessment of political vulnerability.
- Possibilities of expropriation.
- Unfavourable and discriminatory national legislation and tax laws.
- Labour laws and problems.

   f Favourable political aspects
- Tax and other concessions to encourage foreign investments.
- Credit and other guarantees.

C. *Key economic parameters*

   a Population and its distribution by age groups; population density; annual percentage increase; percentage of population of working age; agricultural population as a percentage of total; percentage of population in urban centres.

   b Level of economic development and industrialisation.

   c Gross national product, gross domestic product, or national income in real terms and also on per capita basis in recent years and projections over planning period.

   d Distribution of personal income.

   e Measure of price stability and inflation. Wholesale price index, consumers' price index, other price indexes.

   f Supply of labour, wage rates.

   g Balance of payments equilibrium or disequilibrium, level of international monetary reserves; and balance of payments policies.

   h Trends in exchange rates; currency stability; evaluation of possibility of depreciation of currency.

   i Tariffs, quantitative restrictions, export trading, and other entry barriers to foreign trade.

   j Monetary, fiscal and tax policies.

   k Exchange controls and other restrictions on capital movements, repatriation of capital, and remission of earnings.

   l Monetary and fiscal policies and their effect on price trends, interest rates, economic growth, and stability.

   m Other changes in economic policy that affect international business.

Table A.1 continued

D. *Key business parameters*

a Prevailing business philosophy: planned economy, state socialism, socialistic democracy.

b Major types of industry and economic activities.

c Numbers, size and types of firms, including legal forms of business.

d Organisation (proprietorships, partnerships, limited companies, corporations, co-operatives, state enterprises).

e Local ownership patterns (public and privately held corporations, family-owned enterprises).

f Domestic and foreign patterns of ownership in major industries.

g Business managers available: their education, training, experience, career patterns, attitudes and reputations.

h Business associations and chambers of commerce and their influence in country.

i Business codes, both formal and informal.

j Marketing institutions: distributors, agents, wholesalers, retailers, advertising agencies, advertising media, marketing research, and other consultants.

k Financial and other business institutions: commercial and investment banks, other financial institutions, capital markets; money markets, foreign exchange dealers, insurance firms, engineering companies, etc.

l Managerial processes and practices with respect to planning, administration, operations, accounting, budgeting, control etc.

E. *Key socio-cultural parameters*

a Literacy and education levels.

b Business, economic, technical, and other specialised education available.

c Language and cultural characteristics.

d Class structure and mobility.

e Religious, racial, and national characteristics.

f Degree of urbanisation and rural-urban shifts.

g Strength of nationalistic sentiment.

h Rate of social change.

i Impact of nationalism on social and institutional change.

j Value systems.

Table A.1 continued

F. *Framework for industry analysis*

Analysis of industry structure and trends.
a Definition of industry, including major products.
b Size and scope of industry.
c Value, quantity and growth rates of domestic production and consumption, imports and exports.
d Technological state of industry.
e Product cycle and rate of product development.
f Degree of market saturation and maturity.
g Special government laws and regulations impacting the industry e.g. environmental emission controls.

G. *Competitive analysis*

Analysis of major competitors, including:
a Identification of principal competitors, national and foreign.
b Their types of operation, manufacturing, licensing, exporting, importing, and various combinations.
c Channels of distribution and sales organisation.
d Advertising and promotion.
e Brand establishment.
f Pricing policies and practices.
g Productivity and efficiency in manufacturing.
h Financial strength and effectiveness.
i Effectiveness of personnel, labour union policies, and general management.

Performance differentials of company with major competitors and industry, including:
a Rate of growth of sales.
b Market penetration in major products.
c Market development.
d Product mix.
e Distribution channels and sales organisation.
f Servicing, credit and delivery.
g Advertising, other promotion, and brand establishment.
h Pricing policies.
i Profitability and rate of return on sales and investment.

Appendix III   The staff development and training committee approach

Because this concept has been found to be so beneficial on so many occasions, the following notes are provided as additional practical material.

The first essential is for terms of reference that are clear and open-ended enough to leave scope for initiative. Very briefly the terms of reference can be a variation on the following theme:

- To operate as a steering committee
  - or advisory committee to management
  - or advisory committee to the personnel manager
  for all training and staff-development activities.
- To provide assistance and support in the field of needs identification, in studies of third-party courses, and in any other manner that will promote the satisfaction of training needs in accordance with the requirements of the business.
- To promote and encourage methods of maintaining a positive motivational climate within the organisation.
- To develop an increased awareness of the goals of the organisation at all levels.

Other essentials are:

- Regularly scheduled brief meetings based on pre-announced agendas.
- Specific task assignments to either individuals or sub-groups within the committee.
- Some clear evidence of support by way of feedback from the management.
- Recognition of the fact that the committee is not concerned with policy-making – it is concerned with providing advice and from time to time it may be concerned with recommendations concerning policy.

It is of course concerned with providing living inputs and with the implementation of policy.

Membership of the committee should in itself be a source of pride and a means of recognition and this is well possible if the level of the members is confined to those with budgetary responsibility, people who are already established as having some initiative and people who are concerned with the principal purpose of the business. In practice this means that apart from the personnel manager, who may act either as the secretary or chairman, the other members are usually heads of divisions or departments.

Practice has shown that eight members is sufficient to provide organisation coverage and if, in addition, the committee has the power to co-opt others for attendance as members of specific task teams, the involvement aspect is further enhanced.

Experience has shown that such a committee can be useful in:

- Providing inputs re needs.
- Pre-selling a change in approach such as the introduction of task-oriented appraisal.
- Checking third-party resources.
- Assisting in the task of the post-interviewing of those who have attended courses and the pre-briefing of those who will attend.
- Structuring internal courses or restructuring given courses.
- Presenting course material within the field of their own speciality.
- Jointly encouraging and developing a change of climate through their own exampled behaviour.
- Drafting both a total training and staff development plan and preparing a budget for it. (In this way both the plan and the costs involved are pre-sold to those who have to provide the participants and pay for their attendance.)

A further point is of course that the members of such a committee are themselves receiving, in a very practical manner, an effective but relatively painless form of management development. Certainly they will themselves have to become familiar with the various tools such as forecasting and manpower planning.

Appendix IV Cross-cultural group dynamics – fragility, sincerity and self-control

One of the basic facts regarding cross-cultural groups is the fragility of the links between the members. In so far as those members are not previously known to each other these groups are usually formed on a first encounter basis and, added to this, is the fact that inherently such groups have a predetermined brief life span. Further, the formation of such groups can, and indeed sometimes should, promote feelings of in-group competitiveness.

It could well be imagined that against the background of such facts there would be some hesitations involved in creating these situations – but what are the rewards?

- Discussion, formal and informal, enriched by a penetrating cross-section of opinion.
- Preconceptions and generalities giving way to new cultural insights and appreciations.
- An experience rather than just an event.
- Feelings of isolation giving way to a general feeling of shared exposure.
- Suspicion replaced by sincerity.
- Problems, once thought to be unique, solved by the experience of others.
- A new awareness of resource inputs.
- A new identity in terms of group membership which lasts long past the life of the group itself.

Added to all these, particularly when the members are drawn from different locations but are members of one company, is the fact of vastly improved business relationships.

As an acknowledgment of the dangers, the pitfalls and the potential for situational difficulties, but at the same time as a denial of the thought that these are insurmountable, the following inset quotation is a reprint of a brief handwritten note distributed to participants at a moment in time when a molehill-sized problem was threatening to assume mountain-sized proportions:

As someone said: problems – even small ones – can be converted into opportunities, and of course, there are those who can't resist the opportunity to preach a short 'sermon?'

(1) What is a group –? A number of individuals with different knowledge, attitudes, and skills, different conceptual and interpersonal effectiveness and different degrees of the motivation to achieve. Strengths of the individuals will differ and tolerances between people in a group are like the springs of a jeepney on a Tagaytay road.[1]

(2) The true strength of a group is its fragility. A group in which the links are not inherently strong has to be a stronger group than the group in which the links themselves are strong, i.e. a group composed of members from different countries may, in this sense, be stronger than the group composed of members of the same country.

(3) A threat to the unity of any group can lead to defensive feelings by some members of the group. These feelings can be highly emotive but the point to be respected is the genuine aspect of such feelings.

(4) The controlling force within any group is the self-control of the members within it; the aids to such control are empathy, consideration and respect for others. There is no implication of weakness here, but there is an implication regarding the intelligent use of strength. Discipline is therefore a matter of self- discipline.

(5) A test of any group is whether or not, within it, all individuals are given the opportunity by the others to share in and resolve its inevitable tensions – both large and very small. The ultimate test is

---

1 A local reference to the seminar environment.

clearly whether or not the individuals can maintain the fragile links after the group has been tested. Put another way, the strength of a group is its ability to *demonstrate* its return to 'normality' after a test.

The result in this case was that the group gained in both harmony and strength and the person most deserving of thanks was the man who quite unwittingly created the molehill.

Appendix V The mirror-centred approach; the manager as a professional; cases for colleagues

The mirror concept

While 'mirror-centred' is certainly not a new concept to psychologists, it has perhaps not been fully recognised as a practical self-development instrument in the field of people development. Recent experience in two of the most potentially significant of the emerging countries has, however, demonstrated that it is a further valid tool for directing self-development effort.

As has been mentioned many times in the text, the emerging countries have the advantage of being able to use – for their own purpose – the experience, the philosophies and the proven experiences of the developed and industrialised countries. The essential skill is to use such material in an open-ended way so that conclusions can be derived rather than given.

The series of illustrations that follow as Tables A.2a–A.2n are extracts from a mirror-centred approach that has been devised from the writings of some of the most famous and well known – and most provocative – writers in the field of modern management. The application approach in this case is to show these illustrations, as transparancies or slides, as an integral part of management courses. While the transparencies or slides contain their own apparent truths, some explanation can lead the participants to draw their own conclusions about themselves.

One vital aspect in using this technique is to make clear that the mirror demands self-reflection. It has to be stressed that the title 'Manager' does not in itself denote the ability to manage – nor does it entitle the holder of the title to stand off and criticise. The 'mirror concept' has to be seen as an inner exercise in self-assessment. The lecture, discussion or any other approach is best, for the time being, discarded and, for example, the individuals in the group can be asked to consider the face they see in their morning mirror – a comparatively light-hearted approach at the beginning of such an exercise can serve the purpose of introducing a change of mood, and at the same time it also provides a point to return if the self-reflections are seen to be proving too revealing for any particular participant.

When handled with care it is suggested that this mirror-centred technique provides an ideal method of structuring the open-ended presentation of self-reflective inputs. Used with a perceptive group it can be the ideal means of promoting a sense of self-learning and self-development.

Two further follow-up aids are also provided. 'The manager as a professional', when presented as a home-study handout, provides additional reinforcement of the concepts. Even if the self-rating exercise is only mentally carried out, the mere act of reading the material with its various inbuilt repetitions must have learning value.

'Cases for colleagues' adds other dimensions and can be presented immediately following the self-awareness inputs from the mirror-concept presentation. Here three cases are provided and, as is suggested in the employee-counselling case in the next appendix, the situations and content can be readily localised. Against reality-based backgrounds the added dimensions include acknowledgment of the fact that problems can and do exist and that they are discussed between colleagues – with the further understated comment that such discussions can be made positive for the organisation. This then becomes an instant feedback to the 'Nature of criticism' in the mirror-series.

Table A.2a Impatience as a virtue

The effective leader is often impatient—not with the weaknesses of others but with their unused potential. He is also impatient with himself and is constantly looking for new ways to turn activity into results. He is impatient for positive goals-oriented achievement.

J. D. Batten

Table A.2b Impatience as one of the criteria in selecting potential managers

Such a criteria list may include the following:
1 Impatience for results.
2 A sense of purpose.
3 A positive approach to problems.
4 A feeling that a problem can be solved until it is proved otherwise.
5 Practical judgement and a sense of balance between men, money, machines and materials.
6. The ability to question under the headings of what, where, why, who, when and how.
7 Courage and frankness.
8 A knowledge that all people need recognition, belonging, security and opportunity.
9 Acceptance of the fact that all projects of any significance involve planning, organisation, co-ordination, direction and control.
10 A tough, durable mind that refuses to dissipate mental, physical and emotional energy on negative thinking.

J. D. Batten

Table A.2c   One man's philosophy

- Be sincere. Remember that real warmth and graciousness can't be cultivated as long as you are concerned primarily with yourself.
- Give earned compliments freely. Accept earned compliments graciously.
- Don't blame anyone else for what you are not—but be grateful to those who have helped you to become what you are.
- Have the courage to change what can be changed, the sincerity to accept that which can't and the wisdom to know the difference.
- Be honest with others—and yourself.
- Refuse to let your mistakes inhibit you. Be grateful that they show you what not to do in the future.
- Remember that you gain confidence and courage every time you face a situation that you were previously afraid of

J. D. Batten

Table A.2d   Sarcasm – expedient for the weak

The habitual use of brittle, witty sarcasm, of 'perfect squelches', has no place in the productivity climate. The manager who feels impelled to meet situations in this way is usually taking a path that requires no courage.

Label sarcasm for what it is—a gutless expedient of the weak personality.

It takes much more courage to give the other man a bit of counsel which helps to develop him in some way. Wholesome humour and facetious remarks can often lighten and stimulate a grim meeting. Humour, in fact, is important, but the question should always be asked, 'Will it do something for him or to him?'

J. D. Batten

Table A.2e   The nature of criticism

The nature of criticism is fundamentally important in the
process of change and in the way in which we make other
people make things happen. Criticism that hurts unnecessarily
and without purpose will never move people to action. Criticism
without explanation will get only a negative reaction. A time of
criticism can also be a time of stimulating motivation and can
be used to spark off innovation and generate constructive
thinking. Criticism of the company is another popular activity
in all companies and comes in two main streams—healthy and
unhealthy. Unhealthy in this context refers to that brand of
criticism which is uttered only for the sake of criticising. It
tends usually to come from those who are least successful in
achieving their own goals and the most unfortunate aspect of
it is that those who indulge in it seem not to know how
transparent they are.

Table A.2f   The cynic

Management is referred to by some as being equivalent to
politics. The man with little success seems always to refute the
necessity for ability in his more able colleagues. Such statements
tend to come from frustrated egotists who imagine that their
faith in their own efforts is sufficient reason for career success.
To these people, time, accomplishment and change have little
positive meaning. Every company has its share of people who
hide their own inadequacies behind cynicism. One wonders
whether they are problem-oriented or opportunity-oriented.
They are certainly not profit-oriented. Too often the cynics and
critics are really basically only concerned with impressing
themselves with the validity of their own statements.

Table A.2g Symptoms of the little man

1 He is wrapped up in himself and his own interests.
2 He has many fears—for example, that people will take advantage of him.
3 He makes the simple seem complex—so it usually is.
4 He thinks of the easy as difficult and the difficult as impossible. Again, they usually are.
5 He thinks in terms of actions rather than end results.
6 He accepts others' ideas with reluctance, if at all. When he does, he may represent them as his own.
7 He often wants something for nothing.
8 He is critical of others' weaknesses and seldom acknowledges their strengths.
9 He lacks a real and abiding faith in himself or in anyone else.

J. D. Batten

Table A.2h Managerial growth factors

Profit contribution
Skill as a planner
Rating as a person
Spark—ability
Educational growth
Mastery of time
Score as an innovator
Problem-solving capability
Decision-making
People ability
Priority-setting
Skill as a motivator
Task-setter
People-Development skills
Rating as a delegator
Skill as an appraiser
Staying power

Courtesy of the Dartnell Corporation

Table A.2i   Let yourself go

The prevalence of drawn-faced people in business is too great.
Many executives with deep knowledge and good intentions
are currently inhibiting growth and innovation in their
departments or companies simply because they themselves are
inhibited as individuals.

When you are inhibited you hold yourself back; you fail to
give freely of your energy, enthusiasm and knowledge. You
can be highly educated and thoroughly experienced and still
not know how to open up and be creative and bring new
ideas to life.

Some of the stumbling blocks to letting yourself go are:

FEAR	— of failure, of ridicule, of superiors and of subordinates.
PRESSURE	— to conform, to bend, to meet impossible deadlines.
TIMIDITY	— reluctance to face up to challenge.
PERFECTIONISM	— the urge to do it the one best way or not at all.
HABITS	— repetitive actions and patterns.
ATTITUDES	— based on the past and the *status quo*.

J. D. Batten

Table A.2j Help others to let go

Contrasting attitudes are based on a management climate which provides people with opportunities to stretch and develop their abilities, with identification through communication and with a feeling of shared effort.

The essential point for the manager to remember is that the paralysis of indecision always has a cause and part of his task is to discover the cause and create an environment within which the causes can be removed. Such an environment is characterised by a feeling of creativity, openness, frankness, good listenership and by emphasising people's strengths.

J. D Batten

Table A.2k Your staying power

This quality is one of the most vital ingredients of executive success. The alternative is the manager who is prepared to back down from a problem or project at the sight of the first really tough obstacle he encounters.

The manager who sizes up a task with completion in mind has a great advantage over the person who finds almost every task difficult and every difficult task impossible. It is perhaps this difference which distinguishes the outstanding leader from the run-of-the-mill-manager.

Do you ever start projects with a spurt of enthusiasm that quickly fizzles when you view the difficulties involved? When you are fully convinced that an idea or project is worthwhile and profitable, does it take the fires of hell to swever you from your purpose? Do you always manage to stay rational, calm and objective when the going is rough, and when the opposition is both fierce and unreasonable? How often, by virtue of your positive attitude, are you able to convert the scepticism of others to optimism? For this trait is the mark of a real leader.

Courtesy of the Dartnell Corporation

Table A.21 Wisdom

Care should be taken to select men of demonstrated wisdom for management positions. Wisdom can be judged by:

(A) Evaluating results:

- Has the man developed and motivated people?

- Has he achieved results through others?

- Does he acknowledge the help of others?

- Has he made sound, appropriate decisions even when the facts were sparse?

(B) Evaluating the man:

- What are his strengths and weaknesses?

- How realistic is his own self-appraisal?

- What are his basic goals in life?

- What are his values?

- Has he demonstrated the guts to stick up for his values

- Does his concept of management reflect wisdom and a tough-minded approach?

J. D. Batten

Table A.2m   Habits to be resisted

1. Using bluster and threats instead of firm, consistent requests.

2. Pulling rank instead of facing up to a problem and talking it out.

3 Firing people as a first resort prior to attempting to build them.

4 Dealing with a subordinate on the basis of what he did wrong rather than what he should do that is more nearly right.

5 Telling others your problems rather than your solutions. Buck-passing requires no courage whatsoever and certainly doesn't meet the requirements of logic.

6 Evading a particular discussion or action because it is painful to you. Frankness is often avoided for this reason rather than a genuine desire to spare the other person. The cold facts are that the other person will almost always benefit from frankness if it is genuinely intended in his best interests and tailored to fulfil his individual needs for recognition, security, opportunity, and belonging.

7 Using sarcasm and oblique witticisms to squelch others rather than an orderly, sympathetic approach to achieving a solution.

8 Agreeing with others simply because it is more expedient.

9 Sticking to the *status quo* because change takes time and energy.

10. Other understandable temptations to take the easy way out.

J. D. Batten

Table A.2n The first step to counselling others is self-knowledge

Before discussing the career problems of others, and in particular before discussing those problems with others, it is important to first know yourself:

- In your estimation what is the extent of your own potential?

- What are your goals for the next five, ten, fifteen years?

- What are your shortcomings?

- What are you doing about your own development?

- Are you afraid to fail?

- Are you afraid to succeed?

- Are you motivated?

- What motivates you?

- Are you in the right position to achieve your goals?

- What sacrifices are you not prepared to make for the sake of your career?

- What particular habits are most characteristic of you?

- Are you as healthy as you would like to be?

- Are you able to listen?

- Are you honest with yourself?

- Do you respect yourself?

- Do you enjoy life?

The manager as a professional

This is a self rating series of 100 key points that have been collected from the widest possible variety of resources.

A professional manager is a manager who has learned the difference between amateurism and desophisticated application of known and tested techniques and who can define his own tasks and the tasks of others without the ambiguities usually associated with professionalism.

The points are self-rated 1–7.

A professional manager:

1 Knows that he must be a creator of circumstances rather than a victim of circumstances.

2 Realises that management is a unity concept but that it is necessary to understand the components of managing in order to analyse performance.

3 Is concerned with achieving positive results through people rather than with having only happy people.

4 Concentrates his attention on problem-prevention rather than problem-solving.

5 Appreciates that he will become increasingly incompetent in his technical skill and must become increasingly competent in his people skill and be able to use that competence in his personal counselling.

6 Understands that morale means willingness to work well rather than 'happiness'.

7 Has the courage to be honest.

8 Knows that the quality of the feedback that he receives is directly related to his own skill as a communicator.

9 Before he claims to be a manager, appreciates the depth of meaning of the terms controlling, planning, motivating, co-ordinating and organising.

10 Knows his objective and how it relates to the overall objectives.

11 Knows how to sub-divide the work content of his objective among his subordinates.

12 Can recognise when the need for personal guidance, training or corrective action exists within his group.

13 Can establish clear lines of authority and responsibility for his people.

14 Can together with his people determine what the achievement levels for each of them should be.

15 Knows that problems should be solved as closely as possible to the problem.

16 Knows that his inputs relating to problems should come from people who are aware of the problem details.

17 Recognises the value of analysing problems before discussing solutions.

18 Has a system for recognising the degree to which his objectives are being achieved and has available the appropriate corrective measures.

19 Knows that effectiveness is the central issue in managing.

20 Is aware that having the knowledge is secondary to the ability to put knowledge to effective use.

21 Knows that managerial effectiveness is output-related and that it is something a manager produces from a situation by managing it appropriately.

22 Recognises that he should be aware of his own effectiveness not only his own efficiency.

23 Is aware of the danger of labelling people and of the lasting effect of such labels.

24 Knows how to read total situations and knows how to manage change.

25 Knows that behaviour and situations are related by his type and style of management.

26 Is honest with himself and has the courage necessary for self-analysis.

27 Is really interested in his own self development.

28 Realises that criticism can be motivating.

29 Has the wisdom to give credit to others.

30 Is aware of the need to utilise the strengths of his people and to develop their weaker points.

31 Knows that people can only be appraised against the background of their jobs.

32 Is aware of the need to set realistic individual goals for his people which can be used as yardsticks in performance assessment and appraisal.

33 Knows that a sense of achievement is the best motivator and that to provide it he must provide

recognition to his people and be aware of their need and desire for growth and fulfilment.

34 Provides promotion opportunites for those who have the capacity to take advantage of them.

35 Realises that his example will be a critical factor in the development of his people.

36 Knows that while most people have the capacity for self-improvement it will only happen if their abilities are stretched.

37 Is able to view his objective with its completion in his mind and is persistent in his pursuit of that objective.

38 Remains calm, rational, reasonable and consistent in the face of difficulties and stress.

39 Expects excellence and pursues it.

40 Stimulates innovation by thinking in terms of change and sets priorities to direct energies to the key result areas.

41 Understands the skill of empathising or being able to see situations as others see them.

42 Encourages people to share any information that may be helpful to others.

43 Knows that work can only be meaningful if his people know why they are doing what they are doing.

44 Knows that fear of failure, desire to conform and reluctance to face challenges are indicators of weakness and that he should look for such indicators in his own behaviour.

45 Understands the significance of and practises good listership.

46 Develops his subordinates to the point where they are able to influence him.

47 Appreciates that part of his task is to influence his manager.

48 Has the ability to discipline.

49 Realises that the routine work that is part of his responsibility can only be put to one side when it is completed.

50 Is not afraid of high visibility, of being the focus of attention or of criticism.

51 Gives both information and consideration to others when scheduling meetings.

52 Follows up both in a general sense and, having set deadlines and due dates for completion, in a prescribed sense.

53 Is aware that people not performing well in one position may perform better in another position.

54 Transmits his enthusiasm.

55 Identifies and resolves the dissatisfactions of his people.

56 Realises that his people's need for self-respect and dignity is not so different from his own.

57 Recognises the importance of co-ordinated activity with other managers at a similar level.

58 Is able to see beyond the immediate objectives.

59 Knows that negative thinking dissipates mental, physical and emotional energy.

60 Knows that challenge and motivation have to be sustained by task-setting, by providing encouragement, by positive review and by appropriate awards.

61 Knows that he is part of the organisation and in criticising it or in allowing such criticism he is in part criticising himself.

62 Is not afraid of conflict and prefers to handle it face-to-face whenever possible.

63 Knows how and when to say thank you.

64 Understands that sincerity cannot be a matter of pretence nor can it have real value as long as a manager is primarily concerned with himself.

65 Gives earned compliments freely and accepts earned compliments graciously.

66 Refuses to be overly inhibited by his own mistakes and recognises that they show what not to do in the future.

67 Knows that confidence and courage are increased by facing problems that others may be afraid of.

68 Knows that no management technique is a panacea and appreciates that his implementation of the technique is the critical factor.

69 Demonstrates his pride in his people.

70 Recognises the wisdom when assigning work, particularly to those with little experience, of explaining the significance of what has to be done.

71 Knows that management is fundamentally concerned with making things happen.

72 Knows how to convert problems and opportunities into specific objectives.

73 Gathers facts before making decisions.

74 Is aware of the destructive aspects of shouting, cynicism and sarcasm.

75 Remembers the impatience of his own youth when counselling or commenting on younger staff.

76 Does not make people decisions based on reasons of expedience or convenience.

77 Finds satisfaction in helping others to achieve their goals.

78 Understands that while the *status quo* should only be changed with caution it should not alter the fact that change is the essence of progress.

79 Accepts the fact that all people are different and therefore require to be treated in a different way.

80 Knows that he can avoid neither the exercise of authority nor the responsibility for what happens.

81 Recognises the skill content of interviewing and understands that because fundamental character is unlikely to be greatly changed by task, training or promotion, he must know exactly the specification of the man he is seeking.

82 Understands that successful delegation is valuable to himself and to his people.

83 Knows that the first step in overcoming barriers to communication is recognising the barriers.

84 Knows that communication is concerned with ensuring that people know what to do and with giving them the will to do it well.

85 Knows that development of people is a normal part of his task.

86 Knows that the title of manager does not carry with it the skill to manage or the ability to lead.

87 Knows that trust and respect have to be earned.

88 Is not afraid of exposing his opinions.

89 Helps other people to help themselves.

90 Makes an effort to understand the emotions and ambitions of others.

91 Judges his own efforts according to harder criteria than he judges those of others.

92 Is aware of other people's dependance on his judgement and on his integrity.

93 Knows that, while frankness can sometimes have disintegrating effects, he must, for the sake of others, be as frank as possible.

94 Seeks opportunities to use his initiative.

95 Has the capacity to be competitive both for himself and for his people.

96 Knows the potential capacity of his people and knows his own and their limitations.

97 Can concentrate, particularly in times of stress, on the critical requirements and the key task areas in any situation.

98 Realises the critical importance of his own good health.

99 Is grateful to those who have helped him become what he is and does not blame others for his own shortcomings.

100 Knows himself and tries to see himself as others see him.

Cases for colleagues

Case 1

Mr A is the Distribution Manager of a rapidly developing company producing motor body parts for the overseas parent company and for the local market. Unlike his colleagues, because of the joint domestic and export aspect of his function, he reports directly to the expatriate managing director. Because of the very different processes involved and because of the continuing pressure of growth there is little communication between the various main divisions of the company. In fact Mr A is one of the few senior people who is able to see the operation as a whole. In his functional capacity he has had to learn to judge and balance the urgency of priorities and in the process has gained considerable respect from his colleagues. Within the network of relationships he has also observed that, in order to remain effective, it is important for him to understand the pressures on his colleagues as well as the pressures on their expatriate managers.

On Monday after reviewing the weekly distribution schedule with Mr B, his sales colleague, Mr B settles in a chair in Mr A's office and takes time out to unburden himself of his frustrations:

'All of my time is spent in meetings with the managing director and the marketing director. The trouble is it all seems so pointless. Their minds are already made up and even though we offer ideas there is not much listening and never any acceptance. My salesmen and the mechanics in the factory know more about the real problems than they do.'

This was not the first time Mr A had heard this problem and in his spare moments he had given some thought to it. Knowing that his colleague didn't really expect advice he decided nevertheless that he should at least try to offer some commonsense guidelines.

Group work: Using the above information as a basis, please present an outline of the advice that you would expect Mr A to offer.

Case 2

On Tuesday, after reviewing the weekly stock inventory with Mr C, Mr A's production colleague, Mr C settles in a chair in Mr A's office and takes time out to unburden himself of his frustrations:

'All of my time is spent in meetings with top management. The technical director keeps repeating that the problems are our responsibility – but how can we solve them if we don't have a long-term plan. Authority we have, responsibility we have, but to do what and go where we have no idea. My people look to

me for a sense of direction and for decisions – where do
I look and what do I tell them?'

Case 3

On Wednesday, after reviewing the weekly damage report
with Mr D, Mr A's accounting colleague, Mr D settles in a
chair in Mr A's office and takes time out to unburden
himself of his frustrations:

> 'The top management is always talking about
> establishing a motivational climate. My accounts clerks
> have been with me for years and they are as good as
> any clerks that you could ever meet in this country, but
> we are fed up with working weekends and staying late
> at nights. This place is a constant paper chase and if I'm
> not careful I'm going to lose my best people. How
> motivated do they expect us to be?'

For optimum value it is suggested that each of the three
small discussion groups be given different cases so that the
final discussion including all groups is confronted with the
three situations.

Case note: The total situation can be changed by removing
the word 'expatriate', by localising the names of Mr A, B,
etc., or by changing the title of Mr A.

Appendix VI   Employee counselling –
a training aid

While the importance of this subject has been emphasised in the text it is felt that it may be helpful to add practical support to that emphasis by providing an outline of a brief eight-hour appreciation programme which has been designed for senior staff and used in a number of countries.

Pre-programme

One month in advance, distribution of pre-reading materials selected on the basis of general interest, stimulation of ideas and as an introduction to the general concepts.

Programme content

- Introduction to the behavioural sciences.
- Reinforcement of concepts already acquired.
- Introduction to the mirror concept – know yourself first.
- Counselling related to the concepts of the Development Gap and Needs Analysis.
- Counselling related to the process of appraisal and to grievances.
- Introduction to the basic principles of counselling.
  - seeing people against the background of their jobs
  - observing reactions and responses
  - understanding the concept of individual differences
  - understanding the importance of 'action images'
  - understanding the influences on behaviour

- understanding the concept of empathy
- understanding the language of counselling and the various questioning techniques.
- Effectiveness related to work output.
- Introduction of job-related appraisal and task-setting.
- Introduction to appraisal interviewing.
- Summary of the basic principles.

As has been mentioned in the text the key point in these types of programmes is to localise the discussions in order to provide a reality base for the observations. Two steps which can be taken towards achievement of this goal are the questionnaire (Table A.3) and the combined role play and case study.

Ideally the questionnaire should be tailored to fit the circumstances but the example provided here could be used to gain initial experience. The questionnaire can either be completed in advance of the programme or completed as an opening segment.

The combination of the role play and case study is used as a device to gain the benefits of both approaches without spending too much time in the course of a relatively brief appreciation programme. Again the situation can be tailor-made but in the case of the example provided here it is a relatively simple matter to change the education details and job titles to suit the particular circumstances. In addition the Mr A and Mr B can readily be replaced by any two frequently occurring local names and the word 'the organisation' can be replaced by the name of the actual organisation or company that is using the material.

While the time suggested for the role play is forty minutes, some separate pre-rehearsal of the 'volunteers' for the parts of Mr A and Mr B can add to the effectiveness of the exercise. This means that the 'audience' can be given the total paper and their role pre-specified as being the small group and plenary discussion of the two-case study questions.

Once again use of the given material may be useful in acquiring initial experience with the technique and, on the basis of that experience, other situations can be presented in a similar manner.

Table A.3 Sample counselling questionnaire

Counselling
Please complete

Name

1 As I understand the term, counselling means ....

....

....

....

....

....

2 My personal experience of counselling situations includes
the following...

....

....

....

....

....

....

....

....

3 Particular points of relevance in this country are ....

....

....

....

....

....

....

4 Particular points of relevance in this company are.................

....

....

....

....

....

....

Table A.3 continued

5 The aspects of counselling that seem to me to be most difficult are..

....

....

....

....

....

....

....

....

6 I would like to learn more about the following specific points ....

....

....

....

....

....

....

....

....

7 I have a good understanding of the meaning of the following terms (Please underline).

Motivational climate	Standards of Performance
Empathy	Task-setting
Needs hierarchy	Development gap
Hygiene factors	Conceptual effectiveness
Motivation factors	Pre-and post-seminar interviewing
Succession charting	Planned mobility

Role play and case study

Note for audience

The role of Mr A is that he is a promising young manager with suspected high potential in the organisation.

He joined the organisation in 1972 having completed two years of university study. His first position was as a job planner in the service department. After one year he became a sales assistant in the Industrial Division and after three years became a Sales Engineer. He has recently been appointed to the position of Senior Sales Engineer responsible for ten sales staff and five clerical staff. He has since been told that if he does well in the position he will have the opportunity to visit the overseas head office for one year and to return as assistant manager of the division.

Enthusiastic at first he has since lost some of his drive, his results are declining and it has been rumoured that he is thinking of leaving the organisation.

Role of Mr A

- 29 years of age
- completed two years of an engineering degree course
- studies stopped because of death of father and the need to assist the family finances, particularly in regard to the schooling of two younger brothers
- joined the organisation with the idea in mind of advancing in the technical sector
- very interested in complex electronics and the practical application of equipment
- enjoyed the disciplined aspect of service planning but still really interested in equipment
- joined the Industrial Division for this reason and although not trained in pricing or selling achieved good results because of interest in reading the technical specifications
- prior to getting married was appointed as a Sales Engineer
- advised of this promotion as if it was a command and

clearly expected that the promotion should be appreciated
- wife pregnant, with complications
- has doubts about the future as real interest is still in equipment and in the technical aspects
- received no training in the management of people but has been successful in personal contacts because of interest in and knowledge of the techniques
- hesitant regarding the future, worried about wife, feels that all the forces are closing in and that the future is being predetermined
- thoughts tend to return to the fact that things could have been different if the university studies had not been curtailed
- feels an obligation to the organisation because, with the rapid progress, the salary level is comparatively high
- has not discussed any of these points
- aware that there is an appraisal process in the organisation and that this seems to have resulted in a good reputation and indications of a promising future
- one indication of this was the information that he may have to spend one year overseas
- wife currently in hospital

Role of Mr B

- 47 years of age
- joined the organisation as a school-leaver
- ten years as a technical installation man, became manager and transferred to the position of manager of Industrial Division ten years ago
- known to have a good reputation as a solid, well-meaning man
- attended several management courses but not too impressed as convinced that management is best learned through experience
- has been enthusiastic over Mr A's sales performance and considers him a promising young man who is usually happy to comply with requests
- surprised that Mr A's performance has suddenly

declined and that he is less attentive to his work
- aware that Mr A married some time ago
- aware of a touch of jealousy that such a young man should be offered such a marvellous opportunity but tries not to show it
- has heard that Mr A is even thinking of leaving the organisation
- must now talk to Mr A and persuade him to stay and get him in the mood to pack his bags for his trip overseas.

Role play commences.
Time allowed, 40 minutes.

Small group discussion

1 From the written material how would you assess Mr B's ability as a manager? Please detail the main points of criticism.
2 Given the situation as it developed and, putting yourself in the role of advisor to Mr B, what advice would you give him prior to his discussion with Mr A?

Appendix VII   The organisation profile approach and the self-declaration form

The organisation profile

One of the techniques mentioned in Chapter 2 refers to the completion of company- or organisation-profile studies. Practical experiences in several countries have proved that this approach can be extremely effective in providing a reality base for discussions and for focusing on solution-orientation. That experience has been deliberately restricted to senior staff all of whom, within the context of their own countries, have had some prior familiarity with the organisation language. In several of the cases the organisation-profile study has also been complemented by a management-style profile study which serves the very useful purpose of both confirming the organisation profile and pinpointing the requirement for behavioural modification and change. In addition the dual profiles provide a concrete and individualised set of directions for self-development.

It is an unfortunate fact that, in order to ensure the validity of the findings, such an approach requires a great deal of research by experience and field testing – but, as is so often the case in these application activities, it is possible to find that other people are engaged in similar approaches, granted that the initial purpose, the location, and the degree of sophistication may be very different.

In this case the example comes form Unigate Ltd, London, who through Mr A. C. S. Savory have kindly given permission to reprint extracts from the article 'Company Profile Questionnaire', which first appeared in the publication *Industrial and Commercial Training* published by John Wellens Ltd.

But, first some notes of caution. Just as Unigate had some particular goals in mind and just as that company did not use the questionnaire universally, it is important to mention that such approaches are best designed according to predetermined requirements and should be custom-made for the purpose. In fact the purpose of presenting such an exampled approach is to provide the initial input material so that an assessment of the value and implications of the approach itself can be made.

Further, in an emerging country situation, with its inbuilt tendency for change, the importance of the approach is not the static result of the questionnaire. Rather it is the use that can be made of the result in order to stimulate discussion and to add a greater sense of direction to the change potential.

Most importantly, it is suggested that in the emerging country context such a questionnaire should be restricted to in-course use. That is, at a moment in time when the climate is concerned with solutions and when the negative aspects of the responses can be converted into self-study of ways and means to make corrections and, at the same time, self-study through group discussion of the prevailing management-style implications and the self-development needs of those present. It is certainly not the intention of such an approach that it be used to unify and standardise complaints.

Used well, the technique, or an adaptation of it, can be an integral part of the change process and an excellent aid to self-development.

Table A.4 Company profile questionnaire

Name .... Section...

In the following questionnaire there are 12 sections, each describing one facet of the way a company operates, particularly regarding its employees. Under each heading there are six short statements of different ways in which a company can be described in respect of that particular facet.

Please tick that description which most closely represents how your company normally operates as it appears to you.

In doing this try to be as objective as possible. Don't think only of how your superior manages you, or how you manage your subordinates, but draw also on your observations and knowledge of how other managers in the Group operate. Try to put yourself in the position of an informed outside observer.

If you want to quality your answer, please write any notes you think appropriate in the Comments box at the end of each section.

Direction

A company needs to develop a strategy for the way it wants to manage its affairs; in other words, it needs some sense of direction and purpose which is commonly understood by all its employees. As a general rule . . . .

A We have no sense of direction or purpose—we go from day to day simply repeating what we did yesterday—crisis management.

B We accept the principle of direction and having objectives, but really nobody pays much attention to it and we still lurch from crisis to crisis.

C We recognise the need for direction and objectives but tend to look outside ourselves for someone to give it to us. 'Why don't they tell us what we ought to be doing?'

D We try to determine our objectives for ourselves, with moderate success, but our operating plans are not always consistent with our objectives.

E We set our own objectives and then make operating plans to fit in with those objectives.

In addition to E above, we constantly review direction and objectives against changing circumstances, and if necessary, we change direction easily and in a planned way.

Corporate ambition/standards

In all companies there are accepted standards or norms about the way the company operates and the way things get done. Some people talk about the general 'tone', 'taste' or 'flavour' of the company, and it is to do with the extent to which the company stretches itself. In general, as a company . . . .

A We have very low, even non-existent standards or ambitions. We are content to consistently do the very minimum that we can get away with.

B We do have some standards but they are of such a low level that we can't possibly fail to meet them. The standards tend to be the same as last year's, and the year before that.

C We have reasonable standards about most things, and try to work up to them but once having reached them we are inclined to sit back on our laurels and make no attempt to improve them.

D We have fairly good standards about most things and a general atmosphere in which everyone tries to reach them. We make efforts to review them and perhaps improve them from time to time.

E We set ourselves standards and targets which are quite stretching and demanding though at the same time realistic. We regularly review our standards against our competitors' and look to see if they can be improved.

F We set ourselves really stretching and challenging standards. Sometimes we don't quite reach them but it's not for the want of trying. Everyone is always looking for ways to improve and to make our company the best there is.

Involvement in setting objectives

In general a typical manager . . . .

A Is not told what his objectives are, or even whether he has any at all.

B Is clearly told what his objectives are, but questions and proposals to amend them are not welcomed.

C Is told what his objectives are and then invited to ask questions about them and sometimes suggest amendments.

D Is asked for his ideas first before his superior decides the objectives and then tells him what they are.

E Suggests his own objectives and discusses and jointly agrees them with his superior.

F Sets his own objectives against the background of the wider Section/Company objectives and lets his superior know. The superior rarely has need to change them.

Co-operation/integration between activities

Typically, a branch or department . . . .

A Is actually hostile towards other parts of the business—there is fierce and destructive competition and even attempts to sabotage another department's efforts.

B Behaves as if it were totally independent of any other part of the business, and takes no account of any possible problems its actions may create for others. Very parochial.

C Is aware of some connection and relationship with other parts of the business, but in practice there is little positive attempt to co-operate with others. The prevailing attitude is exclusively 'Why don't they co-operate better with us?'

D Is aware of the need for co-operation with other branches and departments and makes *ad hoc* arrangements to sort out problems.

E Is very aware of the need and there are regular and on-going contacts with other parts of the business to try to improve the level of co-operation. Departmental interests are sometimes given up for the common good. Commonly there is an attitude of 'How can we co-operate better with them?'

F Works as an integral part of the larger company team. There is a feeling of harmony, co-operation and mutual help throughout and every decision is made for the best interests of the company as a whole.

Employee consultation/involvement
Typically......................

A We see no need for or value in formal or informal consultation with our employees—the management team acts as if it had a monopoly of good ideas.

B We have some awareness of the need but our reaction is essentially pragmatic and a case of only 'consulting' with employees when forced to do so by union pressure or legislation.

C We accept the theory of consultation but, in practice, our consultation takes the form of telling the employees what management has decided. 'Won't keep you long, Smith—I just want to consult you about a decision I've made!'

D Before taking decisions which will affect employees, the employees' views are sought, but this only applies to relatively unimportant 'routine' matters. People generally understand the word 'consultation' to refer to formal Joint Consultative Committee (J.C.C.) procedures.

E There is an environment in which there is day-to-day involvement and consultation going on at all levels both within and outside the formal JCC structure. However, it is still seen as something special and is somewhat *ad hoc*.

F The philosophy of consultation and involvement permeates the whole management style, and the actual methods used are flexible and adapted to the needs of the various parts of the business. There is little need for the formal procedures of a JCC.

Delegation
In general, for routine matters in the day to day running of the business ....

A The boss decides what has to be done, and the detail of exactly how it is to be done. He then gives precise instructions to this effect, leaving little or no initiative to the subordinate.

B The boss decides what has to be done in broad terms, but expects his subordinate to work out the detail of how to do it for himself.

C The boss invites ideas about what needs to be done before making the decision himself, and then telling his subordinate.

D The boss and subordinate jointly agree what needs to be done.

E The subordinate decides what has to be done, but checks back with his boss before doing it.

F The subordinate decides what has to be done and gets on with it, because he knows it fits in with the overall objectives.

Disclosure of financial information
Most employees are interested in the financial performance of the company, or at least, the part of it in which they work.
Do you consider that ....

A We deliberately distort or misrepresent information that we give to our employees.

B We refuse to disclose any information other than that required by law in the annual report.

C We do give out some information, but it is minimal and given only reluctantly and under pressure.

D We disclose information in response to reasonable requests and attempt to present it in ways which can be understood by the recipient.

E We volunteer information and try to present it intelligibly but it is still treated as something of a special event—perhaps only once a year and at the time when the annual report is published.

F We operate an 'open book' policy where financial information and its implications are discussed on a day to day basis.

Environment for developing people
Our general attitude towards training and the development of staff is ....

A Negative—no training or development takes place and any proposals about the subject are firmly squashed as 'a waste of time and money'.

B Discouraging—little training or development takes place and that which does is only done grudgingly after a lot of pressure.

C Toleration—we let a certain amount of training go on providing somebody else organises it for us, it does not cost too much and it does not interfere with the day to day running of the business.

D We are interested in the results of training and make attempts to do something about it. There is token support from top management but in times of financial shortage, training is the first thing to be cut.

E Training is actively supported and encouraged and is seen as a way of improving the business. Real attempts are made to help people apply any training they receive to real work so that it pays off in commercial terms.

F The company initiates and promotes programmes of training and development, aimed at improving the effectiveness of both individuals and groups. Every employee is encouraged to develop himself to the maximum of his ability.

Frankness

When some difficult or unpalatable information concerning an individual has to be dealt with what typically happens is ....

A The information is distorted and misrepresented in order to avoid unpleasantness or embarrassment.

B The information is ignored in the hope that the problem will go away—an 'ostrich' policy.

C The information is leaked into the grapevine and whispered about, often behind the back of the person it concerns.

D Broad hints are dropped in the hope that 'he will get the message'.

E Handling the information is seen as a problem but a deliberate plan is made to bring it into the open and deal with it in a constructive way.

F It is treated like any other piece of information which is more palatable, and dealt with openly and frankly without embarrassment.

Morale/enthusiasm

On the whole the general atmosphere around the place and level of enthusiasm is.........

A 'Anti', depressed, a prevailing atmosphere of 'bloody-mindedness'.

B Dormant, apathetic, 'Can't be bothered'.

C Lukewarm, with just the occasional spark of life.

D Reasonable—"it's just a job, but let's try to do it reasonably well".

E Lively and willing—people generally like coming to work and want to do a good day's work.

F Very keen and enthusiastic—exciting and stimulating—great commitment to doing a good job. People feel about Monday the way most other people feel about Friday.

Attitude to change

In general ....

A We are unaware of change, or the pressures to change until we are forced to recognise it and accept it.

B We are vaguely aware of pressures for change but tend to delay doing anything about it until it is almost too late.

C We react to pressures to change on an *ad hoc* and pragmatic basis—we are a bit like a cork floating on the waves of the sea.

D There is an element of forward planning and we generally cope with change and adapt to it fairly smoothly.

E We anticipate the need for change as much as we can and take action to prepare for it in advance.

F We set out to influence forthcoming changes or the effects of them in our favour.

Risk-taking

This refers to the company's readiness to 'stick its neck out' and take risks.
Typically.........

A We try nothing new and are only concerned with maintaining the *status quo*. Our motto is 'If you don't do anything you can't be wrong'.

B We don't like new ideas, but we will try some and provided there is not much risk of failure.

C We are conscious of the risks of not doing anything as well as the risk of doing something new, but we still err on the side of caution.

D We take opportunities and chances where success is reasonably certain.

E We seize more and more opportunities and with some of them the risk is quite high that it won't pay off.

F We are prepared to 'go out on a limb' for what we believe to be a right and good course of action.

Self-declaration form

On a much less dramatic scale but with more moderate intentions another useful technique originates from Japan.

The Self-declaration Form is similar to the more familiar Attitude Surveys but with some very distinct and meaningful modifications. The three features of the translated example that is provided are, the open-ended aspect of the questions, the personalised characteristic of the total form and the clear emphasis on task. These features are evident from the first question and the built-in compliment to those being questioned invites both involvement and honest responses.

In this case the technique is directed towards individual responses in terms of task awareness, task interest, self-development, job satisfaction, job mobility, needs analysis and organisation awareness. Apart from the value of these inputs two further factors are the deliberately dynamic reinforcement of the form design and the potential value of the total approach as an aid to directed counselling.

While the advantages of the approach will be apparent the key issues are adaptation according to prevailing circumstances and application that is appropriate. Again, the example is intended to demonstrate the possibilities.

In terms of the emerging countries there is little requirement for further desophistication but at the same time there is a clear need for pre-briefing of those involved in responding to such a questionnaire. Task-centred solution-orientation is the fundamental intention and any possible tendency towards only problem-identification is the danger to be avoided.

Table A.5 Self-declaration form

	1978 ....
	Div./Dept.: ....
	Name : ....

I Your present job

1 Please write your five key tasks at present.
   (1)
   (2)
   (3)
   (4)
   (5)

2 When were you assigned to the present job?

3 Of your personality, knowledge, skill and experiences,
   (1) which, do you think, is of use for your execution of the present job?
   (2) Which, do you think, should be improved for your better execution of the present job?
   (3) If you have something to be improved, how are you going to improve it?

4 What has been your target for the past one year, which was instructed by your manager or which you planned to put particular emphasis on?

5 How was the result?
   ☐ Carried out as expected.
   ☐ Almost successful.
   ☐ Not personally satisfied with the result.

6 What, do you think, is the reason for not being totally successful in achieving the target?

7 Do you feel it difficult to execute the present job?
   (1) ☐ Yes. Very difficult and requires real effort for the execution.
   (2) ☐ No. Ideal.
   (3) ☐ No. Not sufficiently demanding.

8. Please write your countermeasures or opinion in the case of (1) or (3) or Item 7.

9. Judging from your personality, ability, which do you think,
   (1) ☐ the present job is most suitable
   (2) ☐ the present job is not suitable.
   (3) ☐ others.

10. In case of the present job not being suitable, please write your expectation or opinion, if any.

Table A.5 continued

II Your potential ability	IV Others
1 Which of your abilities is not being fully utilised in the present job?	1 Please comment on any organisational aspects which could be improved in order to assist you in achieving even better results in the present position.
2 Do you have any idea how to use your potential ability for the present job.	
3 In case of not being able to use it for the present job, for what job, do you think, it will be practical.	2 Please use this opportunity for any further constructive comment you may wish to make to the management.
4 If you would point out frankly the most suitable job in the company, what is it?	
III Training	*Interview record*
1 What kind/type of training, do you think, is necessary for the execution of the present job?	
2 Apart from the present job, please write anything about the training you want to receive, if any.	

Appendix VIII   More language dimensions

Further evidence of added value was provided by a pre-seminar discussion which was in itself as enthusiastic as the participation in the Chinese dinner which provided the background setting. Again the search was directed towards clarity of both meaning and intention. In this case the words at issue were: leadership; effectiveness; and motivation – and not the least interesting point was the degree of debate among the three Chinese-language speakers.

Leadership

Here the points to emerge were that, either by translation or by definition of the translation, the term involved the 'desire of the heart' 心願 and an overtone of 'target' or 'goal'. Taking these two points together 'heart' could be understood as 'human requirements' and 'target' could be seen as 'objectives'.

In this way the translation process became the starting point to a total management philosophy which itself led directly to the concept of 'target' or 'task-setting'.

In addition it emerged that 'desire of the heart' could introduce the concept of 'reading the heart of subordinates' or 'achieving mutual willingness towards the same objectives'. With a touch of imagination this lead on to the general concept of 'integration of interests'.

Effectiveness

Here both the word and the concept were less troublesome

and 'dependable for results' 有效 was agreed as being a reasonable explanation. Again though there is a shade of difference with the definition provided on p. 000.

Motivation

In this case three translations were offered.

The first 激勵 added the dimension of 'encouragement'.

The second 引發動機 , which translated into 'the process of placing a new thought in mind' or 'instigating the will to do', added a breath of the traditional definition of morale.

The third, 設身處地去激勵 , or 'stimulate as if you were himself' added the whole concept of empathy.

The degree of debate and the subtle differences of opinion regarding the translation of these three everyday management words highlighted the essential requirement for management courses to be prefaced by clear local language definitions of the key concepts – particularly for middle-level managers. The discussions also reinforced the need for and the advantages to be gained from not only understanding a local philosophy but, even more, the advantages to be gained from using and finding means of integrating with that philosophy.

In this particular case, as well as in the case regarding the Korean language mentioned in the text, it was agreed that that was room for considerable further debate. As both a means of learning and as a step towards greater clarity of intention it was suggested that 'Identifying the mutual understanding of the terminology' would be an ideal initial step in concept introduction for senior staff.

Appendix IX   Multi-country seminar scenario example

As is mentioned in the text 'cross-cultural applicability' is ambitious terminology – but it is a feature of shared learning and shared experience.

The scenario that is provided here is an extract from a practical example that has been applied on four different occasions within a total complex of twenty-one developing countries. The exampled key points are derived from actual situations and an effort has been made to make the scenario motivating to the organisers.

Also useful as a learning aid, the scenario can be readily converted for in-country or in-company purposes.

Table A.6   Multi-country seminar scenario

	Steps	Key points (examples only)
A	Assume that a decision has been made that a seminar could be conducted.	
B	Set seminar theme and objectives	1 To improve participants' understanding of the organisation's management practice.
		2 To confront participants with the point of view of general management in matters of marketing, finance and accounting, and human relations.
		3 To demonstrate the required depth of field of a manager's knowledge.
		4 To stretch the participant's abilities and tolerances to stress.
		5 To provide greater insights into the countries represented.
		6 To provide opportunities for individual exposure as well as shared effort.
		7 Seminar theme and objectives could equally be in more defined field but needs to be specified at this point.

Table A.6 continued

C	Establish qualifying standards for participants.	1	Position responsibility equivalent to a set level or above or for those with an expected equivalent end level.
		2	University graduate education or the equivalent in terms of experience, knowledge and current position.
		3	Budgetary responsibility in the current position
		4	Sufficient fluency in both spoken and written English.
		5	Willingness to work prior to the seminar.
		6	Willingness and ability to participate in the seminar discussions.
		7	Receptivity of new learning.
		8	Where particular skill in any discipline is required it could be detailed at this point.
D	Establish seminar method.	1	Input content from: (a) lectures (b) group discussion (c) guided reading (d) utilisation of experience.
		2	Interaction through exposure to case studies.
		3	Exposure and participation through reporting method.

Table A.6　continued

		4 Stress maintained through demands on time.
		5 Participation approach the fundamental element.
		6 Provide for relaxation.
E	Check availability of appropriate speakers.	1 Utilise all sources.
		2 Maintain high standard of inputs.
		3 Meet personally to discuss main seminar theme.
F	Determine facility requirements and locate.	1 Isolated from a local office environment.
		2 Either with own, or close to alternative, source of secretarial/clerical/copying, etc., aids.
		3 Preferably with suitable accommodation at same location.
		4 With comfortable, well lit conference room with all normal conference room facilities including good acoustics.
		5 Sufficient discussion rooms.
		6 Cafeteria with sustaining food.
		7 Support facilities such as laundry and other services.

Table A.6 continued

		8 Check all sources of potential seminar interruption and all sources of potential personal discontent that could distract attention from the learning situation.
G	Select alternative dates.	1 Bear in mind all contributing sources. 2 Check flight schedules. 3 Look ahead 4−5 months.
H	Establish a seminar budget framework and estimate a cost precalculation.	1 Estimate possible number of participants. 2 Design budget framework utilising known facts regarding (a) accommodation including meals (b) honorariums (c) materials, including stationery, copies and copying (d) refreshments (e) facility costs including special services (f) incidentals including presentations, dinner, picture-taking, certificates, transportation and other depending on circumstances. 3 Calculate cost per person per day.

Table A.6 continued

I	Confirm with appropriate authorities that the seminar will proceed. **DECISION TO PROCEED WITH SEMINAR**	1 Ensure support from the designated official controlling organisation. 2 Appoint organisers who have the authority and responsibility to act. 3 If considered necessary set limits to the authority of the local organisers and discuss.
J	Design a time sequence for events leading up to the seminar. **SEMINAR DATE MINUS FOUR MONTHS**	1 Select a date 4 months in advance of the date of the decision to go ahead. 2 Confirm facility booking. 3 Finally select and pre-brief all speakers. 4 Confirm seminar method. 5 Design seminar programme. 6 Design a seminar logo to be used in all mailings.
K	If more than one local organiser is involved allocate responsibilities.	1 Put responsibilities in writing. 2 Ensure communication between organisers and with controlling organisation.
L	Invite participants from and through the appropriate organisation channels. **SEMINAR DATE MINUS THREE MONTHS**	1 Advise the objective. 2 Advise qualifying standards and selection method. 3 Advise seminar method.

Table A.6   continued

			4 Attach programme.
			5 Advise maximum cost per person also mentioning travel cost and ultimate method of charging.
			6 Advise necessity for pre-seminar work.
			7 Motivate organisations to participate by being professional in approach.
			8 Set time limit for replies within 14 days of receipt of invitation.
			9 Letter of invitation to be received 3 months prior to the seminar date.
			10 Request full bio-data on each nominated participant.
M	I	Local organisers to pre-schedule and prepare all mailings to participants. **SEMINAR DATE MINUS THREE MONTHS**	1 Pre-reading to be mailed to participants and their managements as soon as participants' names are known.
			2 Avoid de-motivating effect by pre-mailing too much content at one time.
			3 Motivate by sending in stages and build up interest by enclosing host country and facility publicity.

Table A.6   continued

		4 Include details regarding seminar programme and method.
		5 Demonstrate high standard, and therefore expected learning level by providing details of speakers.
		6 Advise of likely problems and their solutions such as visa difficulties, airport meeting service, clothing requirements etc.
		7 Underline the fact that it is a working seminar and that golf clubs are not part of the seminar package.
II	If pre-work as well as pre-reading is intended send details to participants.	1 Details to reach participants with copies to their managements 6 weeks before the seminar date.
		2 Details to be sufficiently broad to allow flexibility of interpretation and to require some local research.
		3 Pre-work to include country as well as company information and where possible to relate the two.
		4 The result of the pre-work should be designed to hold the interest of all participants.
		5 Effort should involve participants from each country in a group effort.
		6 Additional individual assignments could be considered.

Table A.6 continued

N	Local organisers to examine all related contingencies. **SEMINAR DATE MINUS TWO MONTHS**	1	Related matters to be reviewed and time sequences 2 months prior to seminar date.
		2	Question necessity for opening ceremony, decide format and arrange.
		3	If appropriate arrange for media coverage of the fact that a seminar is being conducted, of personalities involved, of any content where publicity may be desirable.
		4	Arrange for wording of and printing of the certificate of accomplishment.
		5	Arrange presentation for speakers, participants and host country.
		6	Arrange for relaxation opportunities during the seminar.
		7	Outline content of seminar kit.
		8	Pre-print all known hand out material.
		9	Check all speakers re their printing requirements, their film requirements, the projection requirements, and any other service requirements prior to, during, or following their presentation.
		10	Check on location publicity opportunities such as flags, banners, daily bulletins, etc.
		11	Confirm accommodation arrangements.

Table A.6 continued

O	Review by local organisers.	1	Major review one month prior to seminar.
	SEMINAR DATE MINUS ONE MONTH	2	Review seminar programme against the objectives, the quality of the speakers and the timing and provide for emergencies by arranging short term alternatives such as short management games.
		3	Review seminar facilities and secretarial and other services.
		4	See all speakers and review the theme continuity, participation, and the availability of necessary aids.
		5	Review all mailings.
		6	Review possible food problems and arrange alternatives.
		7	Review arrival schedule of participants and review possible visa or transportation difficulties.
		8	Review budget.
		9	Check availability of all bio-data of participants.
		10.	Arrange final dinner.
		11.	Arrange for pre-purchase of any local items of clothing or art or arrange for on-location sale of these items.

Table A.6 continued

		12	If sightseeing day is part of midway relaxation in the programme arrange for appropriate discounts with tour companies.
		13	Finalise presentation gift.
		14	Print seminar folders, name cards, etc.
		15	Arrange refreshments.
		16	Again reconfirm accommodation.
P	Prepare seminar kit. **SEMINAR DATE MINUS TWO WEEKS**	1	Include copy of programme and relevant details of seminar method.
		2	Include reporting assignments indicating each persons individual responsibility to write brief reports on the content of each speaker's address and to have the reports checked, typed, and circulated to all members.
		3	Include group work assignments and arrange in such a way that groups contain representatives both from each discipline and from each country. If necessary arrange more than one combination within the groups so that the pre-formed groups can take their places without using seminar time.

Table A.6 continued

		4 Include presentation assignments indicating the individual responsibilities for votes of thanks and associated tasks.
		5 Include room assignments.
		6 List seminar facilities and regulations.
		7 To avoid later embarrassment include notes on dress.
		8 Generally avoid being too disciplined and allow for some flexibility for example in finding meeting rooms for groups and in comments on relaxation.
Q	Provide a file for the keeping of handouts and provide other stationery.	1 File should be able to accommodate all notes that are likely to be taken as well as all handouts.
R	Arrangements for day of arrival of participants and speakers.	1 Arrange for assistance with airport formalities.
		2 Arrange transportation from airport.
		3 Arrange dry and wet weather alternatives to avoid anti-climax's on the first day in the environment.
		4 Arrange transportation to the seminar site.

Table A.6   continued

S	Conduct seminar **SEMINAR**	
		1 Thoroughly brief all participants regarding expectations of them.
		2 Provide opportunities to ask questions.
		3 Ensure understanding of the seminar method.
		4 Provide opportunities for constant counselling service regarding any problems.
		5 Avoid over stress but indicate that some stress is inevitable.
		6 Be aware of individual problems.
		7 Minimise discipline.
		8 Take a personal interest in individual as well as group progress.
		9 Be available.
		10 Follow up complaints.
		11 Provide for frank evaluation of results.
		12 Arrange group picture.
		13 Arrange for picture taking to include all individual participants.
		14 Arrange for assistance with departure procedures.

Table A.6 continued

T	Arrange seminar follow-up **SEMINAR DAY PLUS FOUR MONTHS**	1 Write letters of thanks to all of those who participated. 2 To those who may be asked to assist on a future occasion provide some indication of that fact. 3 Ensure that all supporting documents are available for charging of seminar costs. 4 Arrange for distribution of any seminar documentation not circulated during the seminar. 5 Arrange for distribution of photographs. 6 Schedule the forwarding of all follow up material over a four-month period to serve as a reminder to the participants. 7 If necessary conduct a formal seminar evaluation by mail. 8 Obtain post-seminar publicity.

Appendix X   Caution regarding short-term expatriate assignment

While it is not itself a principal point and therefore does not rightly belong in the text of this book, this point is too important to be altogether disregarded.

In the briefest terms the caution in such cases relates to:

- *The potential shortening of both goals and consequences.*
  While the expatriate himself may not be aware of this phenomenon there will be cases where his visions are restricted to the period of time that he is to serve in a particular country.

- *The effects on investment in people development.*
  When vision is restricted the longer-term benefits resulting from the long-term, well-planned development of people may be viewed as short-term costs.

- *The constant need for the local staff, and particularly the senior local staff, to reassess behaviour expectations to re-prove themselves and in fact to re-educate the new arrival.*

The victims of too rapid change are likely to be both the organisation and the local people.

In this case it is a matter of introducing a note of caution without attempting to suggest a detailed solution. Here the solution is 'continuity', but the achievement of this objective is very much an in-organisation matter. In some case the answer may only be a matter of simple briefing – in others it may be a matter of total philosophy that has to be discussed.

Appendix XI   The Ten Commandments for travellers

Rare gems of wisdom can be picked up in all corners of the world. Table A.7 comes from a beach resort hotel, the Samoan Hideaway, which is situated in Vaito's on the Island of Upolo directly south of and on the opposite side of the island from Apia.

While the heading and the reference to 'Ten Commandments' and to 'Travellers' may seem to be a long way from the subject of people development, the gems are contained in 'Commandments' 1 and 4–10. Each one presents a summary guide appropriate not only to all expatriates, but also to all those of whatever nationality or stage of industrialisation who are involved in moving from country to country.

Table A.7 The Ten Commandments for travellers

1. Thou shalt not expect to find things as thou hast them at home, for thou hast left thy home to find them different.

2. Thou shalt not take anything too seriously for a carefree mind is the beginning of a vacation.

3. Thou shalt not let the other tourists get on thy nerves — for thou art paying out good money to have a good time.

4. Remember thy passport so that thou knowest where it is at all times — for a man without a passport is a man without a country.

5. Blessed is the man who can make change in any country, for lo, he shall not be cheated.

6. Blessed is the man who can say thank you in any language — for it shall mean more to him than any tip.

7. Thou shalt not worry. He that worrieth hath no pleasure — and few things are ever fatal.

8. Thou shalt, when in Rome, do somewhat as the Romans do, if in difficulty, thou shalt use thy common sense and friendliness.

9. Thou shalt not judge the people of a country by one person with whom thou hast had trouble.

10. Remember thou art a guest in every land. Yea, he that treateth his host with respect shall be treated as an honoured guest.

Appendix XII   Who is judging whom?

Many foreign managers develop the wisdom to realise that making judgements is often not as productive as taking time out to listen and to learn from situations. In the same way receiving advice can sometimes be a more pleasureable experience than giving it – particularly when it is as well packaged as some of the following 'extracts' that have been collected from many seemingly casual conversations over the years:

- *On the art of understanding and patient listening.*
  In a car on the way to the airport following a not altogether successful visit, the local personnel manager describes a new expatriate manager:
  'He is a very kind man but in such a hurry to hear what he wants to hear. He still has to learn that each man has a heart and each heart has an opinion.'

- *Advice to a minority group agitating for higher incentives.*
  In a very warm office heated by the sub-tropical sun, the personnel manager is addressing a group whose desires for greater benefits had been heightened by a lengthy training visit to Europe which had given them more than sufficient time to compare their conditions with those of their similarly qualified European colleagues:
  'Gentlemen – a tree must be allowed to grow before it can provide shade and protection from the sun – it must be allowed to ripen before it can bear fruit.'

- *On a colleague with too much to say.*
  An aside during lunch:
  'He talks at length at the entrance to the conversation and has no words left when the door is open.'

- *On wisdom in recruitment and management development.*
  Over a drink at the end of a long and trying day a local personnel manager makes his feelings clear regarding that repeated and familiar phrase, that is so often the excuse for almost all failures, which refers to 'the shortage of good local people':
  > 'Diamonds sparkle in the sand but in the sun only a man of experience will see them and only a man wise in our ways will know how to polish each facet to new brilliance – oh, there are in reality many diamonds.'
- *On intra-cultural relationships.*
  A very well educated young manager talking to a senior local colleague at the conclusion of a relatively minor confrontation:
  > '… the fact that I treat you with respect has nothing whatsoever to do with my heart – you only hear my mouth so believe what you want to believe.'
- *On head office.*
  From an older and experienced man just returned from his first visit to the European Head Office:
  > 'How dangerous a small amount of knowledge can be. It's perhaps better to know nothing and to listen more. I've lived here for close to fifty years and the books they read about this country were written by Americans.'
- *After a too critical comment on the local infrastructure.*
  Under his breath while listening to the usual 'this – country is impossible' comment:
  > 'Under the sea all men are brothers.'
- *A general description of the expatriate population.*
  At the end of a senior staff meeting where the expatriate managers had been displaying their knowledge of local affairs and were clearly satisfied that the information available to them was more than sufficient:
  > 'They are too easily satisfied by the volume of their own noise.'
- *On working in a foreign invested company.*
  From several years ago when a local manager was taking great pains to explain the essential difference:

'Working in a foreign company is different. In a local company it is also sometimes raining but it is rain on a thatched roof. In a foreign company it is always as though there is a tin roof. Same rainfall; just more noise.'

● *Again on recruitment.*

An older and experienced personnel manager takes over the briefing task with the new personnel assistant who is destined to be responsible for recruitment in a new factory:

'Look for the heart; the courage to see a new reality. Look for the man able to disagree. Look for pride because he is what he is and knows what he can become. Look for the capacity to love and not to feel small hurts.'

● *On training.*

The training manager reminding supervisors of one aspect of their functions:

'First you must open their minds, then you create a funnel – then pour your knowledge very carefully. You are responsible for what you waste. Not them.'

● *Advice to anyone listening.*

At the conclusion of a meeting when an expatriate manager complained – with apparent good and sufficient reason – regarding the silence of the local managers:

'Be patient with us. We have come a long way without you. Together we will travel forward faster. Who knows who will travel furthest? Who knows the joy of the journey? We can only find out by being comfortable with each other.'

● *On management development – to a high-potential young man.*

Advice from a rather short and thick-set personnel manager (who found it necessary to stand behind his desk on this occasion) to a rather tall and slim young man who was experiencing some difficulty in finding a comfortable position in a too low chair. The point at issue concerned the promotion of the young man without increase in salary:

'You are now like a young tree. Your roots and branches are firm but thin; your flowers bright but

few. This is because you live in a small pot. Now we
are going to put you in a field where the weather
will be varied and where storms will blow. But your
flowers can become many.'

- *Friendly advice.*

To a new expatriate in danger of taking the newly
discovered high-life for granted:

'When enjoying a good meal it is good to
remember the rice farmer.'

- *On staff assessment.*

A local personnel manager comments on the
tendency – sometimes, even the requirement – to
judge people's potential too soon:

'You can only know the heart of another over time
– you only know the temperament of the horse
after a long ride.'

- *On training for the sake of training.*

A reaction to a continuous flood of training
programmes:

'Training to fill time is an exercise in futility.'

- *The generation gap.*

A personnel manager comments on the real wisdom
of the promising young man who is all too convinced
of the fact that the evaluation is correct:

'Youth and age are separated by the art of love. For
the young husband, beauty, sex, 23 and the motions
of mounting passion are the criteria – only age
deepens the sharing of experience, the warmness,
the oneness, the understanding and the ultimate
beauty.'

- *On sincerity.*

A brief but telling comment about the expatriate who
is always eager to shake hands:

'You can't pretend affection.'

- *Again, on the promising young man.*

In this case it is a double-edged sword that cuts at the
young expatriate who is eager to see himself
personified in his junior staff:

'Because the frog in the bottom of the well has a
restricted view of the sky he feels that he can
conquer the planets.'

and, following on an expatriate pre-selection of a number of, so far, unexposed 'crown princes' who are to receive special attention:

'The true strength of a wheat crop is only revealed in a strong wind.'

● *On the manager who knows it all.*

After a particularly voluble session with the self-declared expert:

'Real knowledge makes its presence felt like water in a bottle. When you shake a full or empty bottle there is no noise. The noise only comes from a bottle that is neither completely full nor completely empty. Certainly this bottle is not entirely empty.'

● *On the standard man.*

A personnel manager comments on the very carefully selected and tested newcomer – not unkindly:

'With standard equipment all boats are effective in fair weather – only a storm will truly reveal the good sailor.'

● *On human relations.*

After a fruitless discussion with the manager who cares for results above all else and tends to ignore the people problems that threaten to stop his factory:

'You can't talk about ice with a cicada.'

and later,

'I think he has his own dictionary. He certainly defines things according to his own definitions.'

and during dinner,

'The real reason that he is impossible to help is because he only trusts himself.'

● *On the pretender.*

An aside during a long and tedious period of listening to the recently arrived expert:

'A man who really has knowledge doesn't feel the need to constantly pretend knowledge.'

● *On maturity.*

Overheard during a counselling discussion when a young man thrilled by his past success was demanding new responsibilities and the accompanying job title and name card:

'It's true that in the tropics a young girl soon develops the body of a woman (described in awesome detail). It's true also that she can bear fine children. But in her mind she is still a young girl.'

- *On the technocrat.*

In the car on route to a discussion with another recently arrived factory manager a gentle warning is delivered:

'Perhaps we can make him appreciate that without people a factory is only an inventory of rusting junk.'

- *On timing.*

During a discussion about the planned but perhaps too rapid, departure of a well-appreciated and highly respected expatriate advisor:

'In this country we only eat the dog when all the rabbits are caught.'

- *On appraisal.*

After reading the report of an expatriate manager about his people – a report which contained an unreasonable amount of wishful thinking:

'To go too far is sometimes as bad as going behind.'

- *On sales techniques.*

At the end of a course emphasising product knowledge, sales presentation and overcoming objections:

'It is also true that the smart cat who makes no noise also catches the mouse.'

- *On the ultimate expert.*

From a country where words are not wasted and where pragmatic comment is favoured above exotic repartee:

'His mind is as sharp as a razor – and is just as broad.'

- *On management development.*

In his vote of thanks the local manager interprets the comments of the visiting expert:

'Our task is to further stretch the abilities of those who at present are content to work within the limitations of their capability.'

- *On sincerity*.

  In the same vote of thanks the local manager attempts to clarify the point that it is vital not only to be interested but also to, appear interested:

  'Good cosmetics for a lovely lady are like the good sword for the brave warrior.'

- *On 'perspective'*.

  From a Latin country where too-tight trousers and too-loose shirts are as popular as looking in the mirror – a young man is experiencing some difficulty in understanding the word:

  'It is now clear to me. It is like walking on the street and seeing the movement, the shape and the legs that sets the blood pounding. The back view is enchanting – it must be a pretty one. You walk a little faster until you are alongside. Nothing. It is so sad,'

- *On the transfer of technology*.

  Late in the evening some months following Papua New Guinea's Independence, a chance encounter with a seven-year expatriate in a Port Moresby bar:

  'If only outsiders would leave these people alone – they have enough technology. Let them have time to consolidate what they have. Why keep sending in more ideas and techniques – why keep creating new confusions? These are good people and after a few years when the place becomes home you learn to love them and to hate those who refuse to become involved and can offer only abuse and criticism.'

- and after a short pause:

  'Why is it that each new expert insists on ignoring what the expert before him has achieved? In he comes, secure in his inexperience, blinded by his enthusiasm – mouth open and mind closed. Every time!'

- *The last word*.

  At the completion of a training programme for young managers:

  'Sir, you have a great deal to say about effectiveness and results-related and I think I understand – but why is it that you never talk about strength?'

So much for textbooks?

Reference note

The figures and tables concerning the various influencing factors on behaviour and the communications analogue are not the original concepts of this author. In the first case it is a matter of something read many years ago being brought mentally alive by the demands of a situation in a particular country, and in the case of the communications analogue it is more a matter of impact than memory and once seen, the idea was immediately noted in detail. Unfortunately that was also many years ago and with the frequent moves of both office and home the original source has been lost.

In both of these cases every effort has been made to trace the originators so that permission to reprint could be obtained and the sources acknowledged in detail. Both of these concepts reflect a degree of knowledge and thought that could only emerge from deep practical experience with people and it is hoped that this acknowledgement will serve to bridge the gap of the formal process of prior consent.

In regard to the two sources that are formally acknowledged within the text – Dean Hayes of the American Management Association and Dr John Adair, author of *Training for Leadership, Training for Decisions* and *Training for Communications* – it is felt necessary again to emphasise the potential contribution of their concepts to the total field of people development. Both offer fundamental principles that can be developed to any appropriate level of sophistication.

Within the context of the Appendices, formal reference is made, in Appendix I, to Mr Masaaki Imai and Mr Paul Norbury; in Appendix II to Mr Ravinder S. Dhingra, and in Appendix VII to Mr A. C. S. Savory of Unigate. Again it is felt necessary to underscore the contribution of these gentlemen and to thank them for their co-operation.

In Appendix V, 'The mirror concept', two of the adaptations are made available through the courtesy of the Dartnell Corporation. Both originated in one of their Executive Booklet series, *The Art of Self Appraisal* by W. F. Rockwell Jr. This Dartnell series of brief booklets headed *'What an Executive Should Know about*———' is indeed the source of considerable self-reflective material.

The man most quoted under the heading of the 'Mirror concept' is Mr Joe D. Batten, who is famous for his books *Tough-minded Management, Beyond Management by Objectives* and *Developing a Tough-minded Climate for Results.* Mr Batten's books all express his philosophy of developing the 'whole person', which is so totally appropriate to the creative energies that are so abundantly available in the emerging countries.

This note is not written with the intent of claiming that the remaining portions of the book spring from one mind. As was mentioned in the Preface they are the result of reading and discussion – and practical experience that has been shared with a reservoir of talent that is beyond the reach of any one person.

Finally, particular and personal thanks are given to friend and colleague, John Tai; secretary and right arm, Shoku Kawakami; and to Ann – who in fact made the whole adventure possible.

Index

Accomplishment,
  as a concept 32
  relating situations and people
    2–3, 14, 18
  through authority and
    responsibility 20
  through management functions
    21–2
Action-centred xviii, 5
Adair, Dr John 38, 241
Adaptation 8
Application,
  across cultures 9
  dynamic background xiii, 11
  internationally 9
  Japanese example 29
  of common resources 156
  policies 9
  practices 9
  procedures 9
  systems 9
Approaches,
  committee 31, 176
  concept 31
  concept repetition 31
  conceptual 11

Behaviour.
  basic facts 75
  Batten, J. D. 183–4, 186, 187, 188,
    189, 190, 242
  change 15, 121
  influencing factors 6, 55, 241
  internal influences 6
  interpersonal influences 6
  physical influences 6
  social influences 6

Business cycle 11, 16

Change,
  achievable 11
  agent for 3
  challenge of xv
  climate of xiii
  country implications 122
  desire for 1, 3
  management of xiii
  motivating aspects 135
  of society xvi
  social commitment 121
  speed of 117
  through people xvi, 151
  vision of future 15, 120
Common denominators 8, 29, 152,
    157
Communications,
  analogue 36, 46, 241
  barriers 66
  condescending 2
  cultural differences 38
  definition 60
  dual purpose 61
  exercises, group 59–72
  individual 56–8
  expatriate quality 147
  international 158
  language aspect 35, 116
  meaningful 11
  pre-reading 55
  responsibility for 37
  understanding 2, 46
  value of 65
Community integration 115
  accomplishment 32

dynamic 32
effectiveness 32, 160–1
mirror 181
mutual support 32
output related 32
results related 32
self knowledge 32, 181–99
understanding 158
warmth of 40
Counselling 13, 32, 74, 75, 83, 108, 166, 191, 200–6
Criticism, the nature of 184
Cross cultural applicability 9, 29, 152, 178
Cultural,
added value 160
differences 1, 36, 38, 151, 234

Dartnell Corporation 131
Delegation 87, 130
Desophistication 11, 38, 152
Development, *ad hoc* 27
Development gap 21, 164
Dhingra, Ravinder S. 172, 242
Dynamic concept 32

Effectiveness 24, 32, 160–1
Emotion,
re multinationals xviii
re words 2, 11
Empathy 46, 149, 155, 167
Environment,
and behaviour 6, 55
and culture 5, 40
and education 5, 25, 98, 155
and employment 98
and strategy 3, 137
appropriate norms 34
current capability 4
differences 9
future vision 15
influence on process 16
infrastructural change 5
objectives within 2
Expatriates,
communicating quality 147
life cycle 148
local view 148, 234, 235
motivation 139

planned replacement 124
qualities of 142–7
reasons for 138
short term 231
Expectations,
and change 5, 121
in-built xv
past experiences xv

Feedback 33, 36, 82
Frankness 2

Government relations,
aiding 127, 129
supporting role 155
Group dynamics 178
Growth,
accomplished by people xv
dynamics of 35
pains of 119, 155
people effects 129
perspective xv
projections 25
sequencing 22
training effects 87
vision of 35

Habits, to resist 190
Hayes, Dean J. 21, 241
Highly structured 49–78

Idea injection 33
Imai, Masaaki 241
Impatience,
as a virtue 183
as a selection criterion 183
Implementation phases,
and planning 152
functions and skills 45
language 45
managing 45, 73
three phases 50
Integration of interest 34, 129, 168
Integration of vision 15, 35, 120, 129, 146, 168
Interview,
conversation 74
experience 179, 181
fundamentals 92

guide 93–4
investment aspect 90
job description 94
limitations 91
priority aspect 154
role plays 99, 100
Investment in accomplishment 2
Involvement 32, 79, 82, 114, 117, 155
'Isation' 120, 124, 139

Job description 31
caution 94
responsibility areas 96, 107

Knowledge,
depth 13
desophistication 11

Leadership,
and morale 76
style 3
task approach 38
via example 83, 148
Learning barriers 34
Local legal practice 7, 20, 114
Local practice 7, 20, 114
Localised thinking 33
Localising,
aids to 78, 197–205
planning 125
Look ahead chart 22, 106

Management,
components 12, 17
concepts 31
content 12, 21
culture 40
definition 2, 18
development xvi, 110, 236, 239
functions 19, 21
information systems 116
language 33, 35, 115, 153, 157, 164, 215–16
motivation 76
process 12, 16
strategy 16
unity concept 19
Matrix 26

Mirror concept 181
Motivators 83
Multinationals xviii, 156, 159, 166–8
Mutual support 33

National development 123
National uniqueness 9, 29
Nationalism,
and industrialisation xviii
and pride 14–15
Needs,
analysis 26, 84–6, 163
emerging pattern 25
identification 25, 81
in-context 28
initial strategy 3
inventorisation 109
reality based 13
Need to know 49
Norbury, Paul 241

Optimum sophistication 12
Organisation 22, 23–4
Organisation profile 31
Output related 32

Packaged programmes 4
Performance assessment 107, 108
Personnel department 114
Philips xiv, 166
Planning,
career and succession 103, 110, 163
development 108
implementation 45
linking philosophy and reality 154
look ahead chart 106
national development 122
organisation charting 104
personnel strategy 113
policy announcements 116
three phases 49
Pride 1, 9, 14, 130
Problem identification 118, 120
Profiles,
in-company climate 81
job 42

organisation 31, 81, 207–11
   personal 31, 207

Resource,
   allocation 28
   sharing 33
   utilisation 28, 152, 156
Respect,
   for local situation 5
   for self 1, 168
   for senior staff 80
Rockwell, W. F. Jnr. 242

Sarcasm 184
Savory, A. S. C. 208, 242
Scenario 217
Selective spending 38
Self declaration 212
Self knowledge 32, 82
Sincerity 2, 78, 237, 239
Staff development committee 176
Staff retention 38
Standards of performance 23, 81,
   107, 162
Strategic planning 172
Strategy 3, 137
Support concepts,
   committee approach 30, 176
   consultation approach 31
   job description approach 30

organisation profile approach
   31, 207–11
personal profile approach 31
repetition approach 31
spring board approach 30

Task setting 23, 81, 162
Training,
   business related 102, 154
   cost benefit 102
   government relations 127–31
   local view 236
   panacea aspect 102
   phases 47, 50
   planned implementation 45
   reality demands 87
   via example 47
Transfer of technology 87, 131–5, 138

Understanding,
   common 45
   cultural differences 234
   effort towards 5
   language 33, 46
Unigate Limited 207, 241
Uniqueness 8, 14, 17

Vision 15, 23, 35, 121, 129, 146, 168

Wisdom 189, 234